GREAT MILITARY
DISASTERS

GREAT MILITARY
DISASTERS

General Editor: Michael E. Haskew

Bath · New York · Singapore · Hong Kong · Cologne · Delhi
Melbourne · Amsterdam · Johannesburg · Auckland · Shenzhen

This edition published by Parragon in 2011
Parragon
4 Queen Street
Bath BA1 1HE, UK
www.parragon.com

ISBN: 978-1-4454-6436-7

Editorial and design by
Amber Books Ltd
Bradley's Close
74–77 White Lion Street
London N1 9PF
United Kingdom
www.amberbooks.co.uk

Project Editor: Michael Spilling
Design: Rick Fawcett
Picture Research: Terry Forshaw
Maps: JB Illustrations and Peter Bull

Printed in China

CONTENTS

INTRODUCTION

History tells us that the only certainty in military conflict is that there will inevitably be uncertainty. Planning, positioning, intelligence gathering, strategy, and tactics are essential components of a military campaign and a successful outcome on the field of battle.

Too often, however, the great unknowns, the variables, and the elements of armed conflict that are simply beyond the control of any commander or command, weigh heavily on the outcome of a battle. Regardless of preparation, preponderance of strength, superb training, and coordinated logistics, the possibility of a "water-tight" plan unraveling always exists. Therein lies the risk of battle—the distinct possibility of a great military disaster. A disastrous military defeat may seal the fate of a nation, an empire, an ideology, or a civilization. Always, the stakes are high, and the cost may be measured in the dearest of terms, the lives of men who follow their leaders into the maelstrom of conflict.

Through insightful narrative, detailed maps, and lavish illustrations, *Great Military Disasters* explores a number of the most famous and infamous debacles in the history of armed conflict. Eminent historians provide perspectives on battles, large and small, some of which literally changed the world while others compelled great powers to acknowledge the

limits of their influence or revealed the fatal flaws of personality, pride, or incompetence, the unpredictability of weather conditions, the consequences of confusion during the heat of battle, and the passing of precious time.

UNCONTROLLABLE FACTORS, UNCERTAIN OUTCOMES

No military commander can control the weather. He can only consider the prediction of it, potentially utilize its effects to his advantage, or modify strategy and tactics to accommodate it. At Agincourt in 1415, King Henry V and the English longbow ruled the day as heavily armored French knights became mired in the mud left by torrential rains. While English seamanship and the confines of the Channel contributed mightily to the defeat of the Great Armada in 1588, violent storms pounded the Spanish galleons, compounding their tremendous losses.

At Cannae in 216 B.C.E., Hannibal executed the tactical double envelopment, and the Carthaginian army inflicted a humiliating defeat on the legions of Rome. Unaware of their adversary's intent, the Roman commanders, Consuls Paulus and Varro, failed to recognize the trap into which their forces plunged. Thousands of Roman soldiers perished, and some historians speculate that the slaughter may have been the greatest ever in a single day. Two millennia later, the modern army of France, intent on maintaining control of its colonial empire in Southeast Asia, failed as well. The French military underestimated the determination of their communist Viet Minh foe and foolishly occupied the valley of Dien Bien Phu. The outcome was a decisive victory for the Viet Minh, the end of French rule in Indochina, and the eventual involvement of the United States in the protracted and costly Vietnam

BELOW: CHRISTIAN SAILORS take on their Ottoman adversaries in ship-to-ship fighting at Lepanto, 1571. Superior naval technology in the form of the heavily armed galleasses ensured a Christian victory in a battle that decided the fate of the Eastern Mediterranean.

ABOVE: *FRENCH FOREIGN LEGIONAIRES carry a wounded comrade after fighting at Dien Bien Phu, Vietnam 1954. The defeat at Dien Bien Phu ended French power in Indochina and consolidated Viet Minh control over the north of Vietnam.*

War. In 1993, in the city of Mogadishu in war-torn Somalia, the sharp clash of arms between U.S. forces and guerrillas loyal to Somali warlords, including the harrowing incident referred to as "Blackhawk Down," challenged American resolve amid changing geopolitical circumstances. Somalia remains largely in a state of anarchy two decades later.

OVERSTRETCHED AND OVERCONFIDENT

Napoleon's reach exceeded his grasp during the French Army's 1812 campaign against Russia. Previously everywhere victorious, the master strategist overextended his supply lines and could not adequately sustain his forces as the retiring enemy employed a scorched earth policy. Marching thousands of miles to Moscow, the emperor found that he

had achieved virtually nothing, and the bitter winter retreat of the French destroyed a great army.

In the summer of 1942, Adolf Hitler's Nazi juggernaut had yet to taste defeat on the Eastern Front. The Führer's obsession with capturing Stalingrad, however, proved to be his undoing. Although his forces occupied the city, a ring of Red Army steel prevented escape, resupply, or rescue. The German Sixth Army was destroyed, signaling the beginning of the end for the Third Reich. To paraphrase the philosopher George Santayana, Hitler had failed to remember the past and was, therefore, doomed to repeat it.

The poetry of Alfred, Lord Tennyson captured the futility, anguish, and heroism of the Charge of the Light Brigade at Balaclava during the Crimean War (1854–56). Tragic though it was for Britain in terms of casualties, the tragedy was heightened by the controversy that followed. Was the decimation of the cavalry force caused by the incompetence of senior commanders, or was the order that launched the fateful charge itself misunderstood in the midst of swirling battle?

When Admiral Zinovi Rozhestvensky and the Russian Baltic Fleet reached the Strait of Tsushima, his warships had nearly circumnavigated the globe, and the commander himself had never before felt the sting of battle. His opponent, Japanese Admiral Heihachiro Togo, employed the classic naval maneuver of crossing the enemy's "T" and devastated the Russians. The victory was so complete that the outcome of the Russo-Japanese War was decided as much at sea as it had been on land. Japan had defeated a traditional European power, and the Rising Sun would come to dominate East Asia for decades.

Despite the carnage of two previous days' fighting at Gettysburg, General Robert E. Lee was undeterred. The Confederate Army of Northern Virginia had yet to be defeated in battle. On July 3, 1863, Lee ordered thousands of soldiers to cross a mile of open terrain and assault the center of the Union army's line on Cemetery Ridge. Those who executed Pickett's Charge gained only immortality. In retrospect, had Lee been blinded by his belief in the invincibility of his army? He had taken great risks before

BELOW: INFANTRY STRUGGLE through the snow and cold of a Russian winter as Napoleon's Grand Armée retreats from Moscow in the winter of 1812.

ABOVE: RED ARMY SOLDIERS of the Soviet Sixty-Second Army advance through the ruins of Stalingrad, December 1942. The city was reduced to rubble after six months of intensive fighting.

and won. At Gettysburg, Lee accepted responsibility, admitting that the fault was his alone.

Other commanders, believing in the invincibility of their armies or navies, have also come to grief. Like Lee, the Crusaders at Hattin in 1178, the Spanish commanders who ordered the Great Armada to defeat in 1588, the vainglorious George Armstrong Custer at Little Big Horn in 1876, and the Allied planners of the ill-fated Gallipoli operation in 1915, each, if for different reasons, was convinced that victory would be theirs. Neither religious fervor, previous successes, greater numbers, nor superior arms is, in itself, a guarantor of victory.

On occasion, time ticks away, and the opportunity to avert disaster or inflict irreparable damage on an enemy is as elusive as victory itself. On the eve of Pearl Harbor, the United States, many believe, received ample warning of Japanese intentions to strike somewhere in the Pacific.

The failure to recognize the ominous signs of an impending aerial attack against U.S. military installations in Hawaii proved catastrophic on December 7, 1941. In hindsight, the deaths of 2,403 Americans might have been averted.

Scarcely six months later, on June 4, 1942, a powerful Japanese naval force intent on the capture of Midway Atoll, met defeat in a matter of seconds. American dive bombers destroyed three Japanese aircraft carriers, and later a fourth, breaking Japanese naval dominance in the Pacific and essentially determining the outcome of the war that ended three years later.

The causes of great military disasters are many. Analyses may reveal both the subtle and the obvious. Discussion and debate will continue, and in some cases, the consequences of disastrous battles are still reverberating across history.

GENERAL EDITOR: **MICHAEL E. HASKEW**

ABOVE: *PRUSSIAN INFANTRY advance at the battle of Sedan, 1870. The French army was beaten by superior German weapons and tactics.*

CANNAE   216 B.C.E.

The double envelopment is a difficult tactic to perform successfully. On this occasion, however, Hannibal's plan worked perfectly and delivered a catastrophic defeat to the Roman army. As a result the double envelopment, or pincer attack, is sometimes referred to as the Cannae Maneuver.

The Second Punic War between Carthage and Rome ran from 219–202 B.C.E. and ended in defeat for Carthage, but the early years of the war were a desperate time for Rome. The Carthaginian general Hannibal Barca (247–183 B.C.E.) launched a successful invasion of Italy by the unlikely overland route, bringing a substantial army containing war elephants over the Alps.

The Roman leadership of the time was not very good. The Consuls who led the armies of Rome were political leaders rather than professional generals. This made some sense, in that the army was a tool of political will, but it led to a number of problems, not least of which was the pressure to win a victory in order to ensure success in the next round of Consular elections. Such pressure was one reason why the Consul Tiberius Sempronius Longus (c. 260–210 B.C.E.) recklessly

CANNAE FACTS

Who: A Roman Consular army numbering 80,000 infantry and 7,000 cavalry under Consuls Paulus and Varro, opposed by a Carthaginian army of 40,000 infantry and 10,000 cavalry under Hannibal.

What: Hannibal lured the Romans into attacking his position. His center gave way, drawing the Romans in while they were outflanked and attacked in the rear.

Where: Near Canosa, in the province of Bari in southern Italy.

When: August 2, 216 B.C.E.

Why: During the Second Punic War between Rome and Carthage, Hannibal wanted a decisive victory to further his campaign in Italy.

Outcome: Hannibal's plan was an unqualified success and the Roman army was shattered.

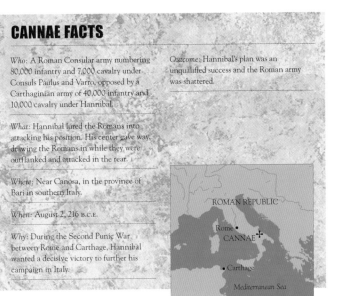

LEFT: THIS ROMANTICIZED EIGHTEENTH-CENTURY DEPICTION *of the death of Paulus at the Battle of Cannae shows legionaries wearing armor that will not be in service for another three centuries.*

sought action with Hannibal's army, allowing his force to be drawn into battle under adverse conditions at the Trebia River. His successors were even more soundly trounced in one of the largest ambushes in history at Lake Trasimene.

DIFFERING STRATEGIES

Hannibal was a clever and skilled general who knew how to handle troops but also, more importantly, how to make war and manipulate his enemies into making mistakes. Using raids or gestures designed to inflict humiliation

ABOVE: *The site of the battle of Cannae today. Otherwise unremarkable, it has become a metaphor for crushing defeat.*

CARTHAGINIAN INFANTRYMAN

Carthage used different types of troops with varying arms and equipment. In the early clashes with Rome, Carthaginian spearmen had strong Greek influences, but changes were taking place by the time of Hannibal's campaign into Italy.

The spearman below shows the influence of contact (and conflict) with Rome. His spear is shorter than it would have been a few years previously, and a large oval shield slung from the left shoulder protects him. By turning to the right, he can place his shield in front of him, though it is not as mobile as a shield carried entirely on the arm. In addition to his shield, a mail shirt, greaves, and a metal helmet with cheek pieces protect the spearman. He carries a dagger or short sword as a backup weapon.

and embarrassment on politically appointed Roman commanders, he was adept at luring them into battle on his own terms.

Hannibal was also careful to separate Rome from her allies, persuading some cities to change sides and others to withdraw from their alliances with Rome. With each defeat, Roman prestige fell ever lower and the Romans' ability to continue the war was seriously impaired.

Rome was forced for a time to adopt a strategy of attrition, hoping that the Carthaginian army would be worn down by nuisance attacks and the fact that it was operating very far from home. However, the Carthaginians kept themselves supplied by ravaging the countryside, inflicting economic damage—as well as the political consequences of Rome being seen as unable to prevent the pillaging.

While the Carthaginian army was admirably handled, the Roman forces were used more like a battering ram. Flanked by allies, the Roman legions were a potent fighting force, but their commanders kept throwing them forward into a reckless advance. Against an unimaginative enemy this was a viable strategy, but a master like Hannibal was bound to take advantage of his enemies' predictability.

HANNIBAL'S PLAN

Hannibal wanted a decisive victory to drive more of Rome's allies away and to push his campaign forward. Although his elephants had all died by this point, he still commanded a powerful force of 40,000 infantry and 10,000 cavalry, who were experienced and confident.

In order to draw out the Romans, Hannibal occupied the supply base at Cannae. When a massive Roman army moved into the area to attempt its recapture, he deployed for battle very close to the Roman camp, daring his enemies to come out and fight. This move was well judged. Two Consuls, Varro and Paulus, commanded the Roman

BELOW: HANNIBAL AND HIS ARMY PARADE through the streets of a captured Italian town. Roman influences are obvious in the armor and equipment of the Carthaginian troops.

army, which numbered 80,000 infantry and 7,000 cavalry. The Consuls alternated command each day. Varro was known to be reckless and so Hannibal chose to goad him into giving battle. In this he was successful; Varro ordered his army to deploy for battle on August 2, 216 B.C.E.

The Romans deployed in their standard manner, with lightly equipped velites (light infantry) in front, backed by more heavily armored legionaries. Allied Italian infantry flanked the Roman contingent. Roman cavalry held the right wing, allied horsemen held the left.

Hannibal deployed his forces behind a screen of light troops, concealing the dispositions of the bulk of his army. His infantry were placed in a crescent formation, bowed out toward the Romans. Light Numidian cavalry were arrayed on the right, with heavy cavalry on the left. Faced with a superior number of better-equipped infantry, Hannibal's center was in grave danger of being driven in. He was not too worried about this. In fact, he was counting

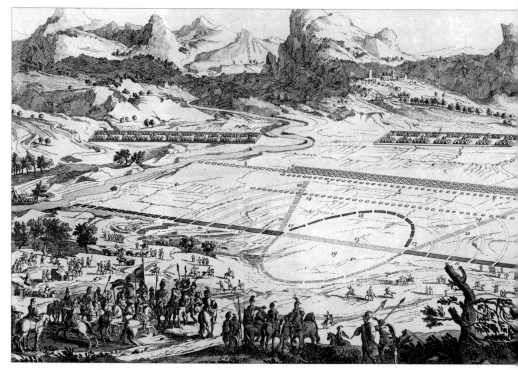

ABOVE: A RENAISSANCE DRAWING OF THE BATTLE OF CANNAE. *Hannibal's resounding victory ensured that strategists and scholars would study his tactics for centuries to come.*

on it. As Hannibal had predicted, the Roman infantry rolled forward, intent on crushing the inferior troops in front of it. The velites pulled back, allowing the legionaries to engage. The crescent of Carthaginian swordsmen was flattened out and then driven in, encouraging the Romans to push onward, deeper into the enemy formation.

In fact, Hannibal had ordered his swordsmen to give ground, though they had little choice in the face of the enormous Roman steamroller that faced them. As the main line conducted its fighting retreat, the light troops that had made up the screen reformed on the flanks and to the rear.

Meanwhile Hannibal's cavalry advanced and encountered its Roman opposite numbers. The heavy cavalry was successful in driving off the Romans it engaged, and was able to detach a sizable force to attack the rear of the Romans' allied cavalry.

DOUBLE ENVELOPMENT

Even as the Roman commanders were sensing victory and committing ever more troops to the center of the line, the light Carthaginian infantry was swinging around to close the flanks while their cavalry attacked the Roman rear. Surrounded on all sides, the Romans were pushed together so tightly that many could not raise their weapons. Some realized in time that their overconfidence had caused them to march into a deathtrap and began trying to cut a way free. Some 8,000 men managed to escape the slaughter. The rest were massacred.

OUTCOMES

Rome committed eight of its own legions and eight of its allies, adding up to approximately 80,000 men. About 55,000 were killed, including the Consul Paulus, 80 senators, and 21 tribunes. Another 10,000 soldiers were captured. Several cities withdrew from alliance with Rome after the battle, and morale in Rome itself fell ever lower.

However, although Hannibal had utterly smashed a Roman army for the loss of fewer than 6,000 men, and achieved a useful political result, he was unable to follow up his victory because he did not have the siege equipment necessary to capture Italy's walled cities. He was thus forced to continue campaigning in Italy. Rome remained undefeated and would eventually return to the ascendant under the

ABOVE: *This nineteenth-century magazine illustration gives an indication of the impact of defeat at Cannae. Shock and despondency rippled through the civilian and military populations alike.*

generalship of Publius Cornelius Scipio (236–184 B.C.E). Hannibal's strategy at Cannae worked primarily because the Romans were tremendously overconfident. They simply trusted to the superior killing power of their legions and stomped forward, intent on smashing the enemy before them. Given recent defeats under similar circumstances it is easy to say they should have known better, but Hannibal gave the Roman commanders a strong incentive to accept battle and to seek a swift victory.

Thus to a great extent the Romans were the victims of a difficult political situation, which forced them into seeking a quick victory. Their own political system was also at fault, sending politicians to face an immensely skilled military commander who knew how to make best use of his enemies' predictability and overconfidence.

LEFT: *Publius Cornelius Scipio Africanus was one of the survivors of Cannae and other Roman defeats. He eventually led Rome to victory over Hannibal and Carthage.*

15

CANNAE

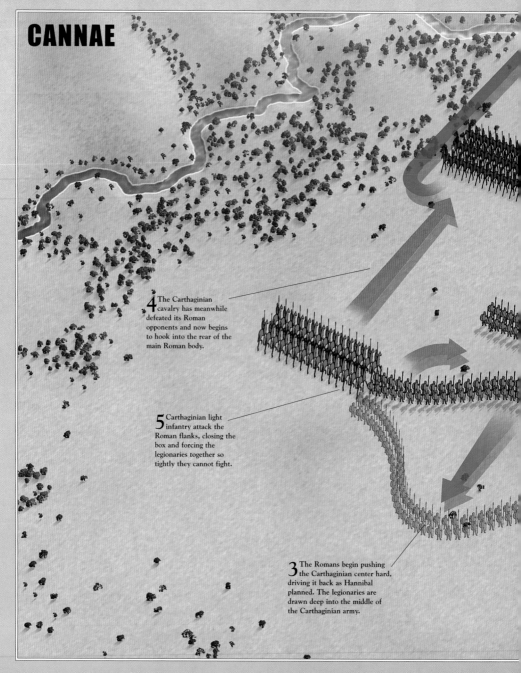

4 The Carthaginian cavalry has meanwhile defeated its Roman opponents and now begins to hook into the rear of the main Roman body.

5 Carthaginian light infantry attack the Roman flanks, closing the box and forcing the legionaries together so tightly they cannot fight.

3 The Romans begin pushing the Carthaginian center hard, driving it back as Hannibal planned. The legionaries are drawn deep into the middle of the Carthaginian army.

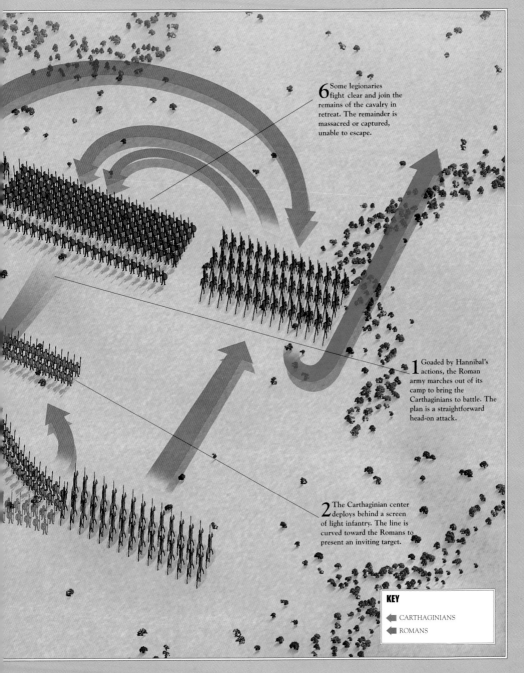

6 Some legionaries fight clear and join the remains of the cavalry in retreat. The remainder is massacred or captured, unable to escape.

1 Goaded by Hannibal's actions, the Roman army marches out of its camp to bring the Carthaginians to battle. The plan is a straightforward head-on attack.

2 The Carthaginian center deploys behind a screen of light infantry. The line is curved toward the Romans to present an inviting target.

KEY

◀ CARTHAGINIANS

◀ ROMANS

TEUTOBURG FOREST

9 C.E.

"Quinctilius Varus, give me back my legions!" wailed Augustus Caesar (63 B.C.E.–14 C.E.) upon receiving the news of a disastrous military defeat in far off Germania. In the Teutoburg Forest, three Roman legions, 25,000 strong, had been annihilated. Augustus feared not only a threat to the Roman Empire, but also the end of 40 years of territorial expansion.

With the pacification of Gaul, the eyes of the empire had turned eastward, toward the mighty Rhine River and Germania. The expanse of the great waterway marked an unofficial boundary between the area of Roman dominion and the territory inhabited by numerous Germanic tribes. Although these tribes were often at war with one another, they also frequently raided and pillaged Roman outposts. Prompted to action, Augustus dispatched

TEUTOBURG FOREST FACTS

Who: Germanic tribes led by Arminius (17 B.C.E.–21 C.E.) versus three Roman legions and support troops under Publius Quinctilius Varus (46 B.C.E.–9 C.E.).

What: A confederation of German tribes ambushed the Roman legions in the dense forest and annihilated them.

Where: Teutoburg Forest, Lower Saxony, near modern Osnabrück, Germany.

When: September 9–11, 9 C.E.

Why: The Germanic tribes intended to avoid domination by the Roman Empire.

Outcome: The Roman legions are destroyed, Varus commits suicide, and Germania remains free from Roman rule.

TEUTOBURG FOREST ✛

GERMANIA

ROMAN REPUBLIC

• Rome

LEFT: IN THIS NINETEENTH-CENTURY PAINTING, *Roman legions under Varus are set upon by Germanic tribesmen led by Arminius in the Teutoburg Forest. The Romans were slaughtered.*

his adopted son, Drusus (38–9 B.C.E.), in 17 B.C.E. to stabilize the frontier, much as Marcus Agrippa (63–12 B.C.E.), governor of Gaul, had attempted two decades earlier. For seven years, Drusus campaigned eastward to the Elbe River, establishing a buffer along the Rhine and forcing numerous tribes to submit. His brother, Tiberius (42 B.C.E.–37 C.E.), extended Roman influence, and by the eve of the millennium most of the Germanic tribes had accepted subjugation.

THE PRICE OF PEACE

The maintenance of an uneasy coexistence with the Germanic tribes required a substantial Roman military presence, which, in turn, contributed to strained relations. The seeds of discord had been sown, and in 7 C.E., Augustus

GERMAN TRIBAL LEADER

This Germanic tribal leader, distinguished by his distinctive winged helmet, wears a tunic decorated with traditional emblems, and leather shoes with long thong straps. He carries a heavy broadsword at the waist. During the campaign, which culminated in the Battle of the Teutoburg Forest, Germanic tribes were able to put aside their differences to fight against the Romans, a common enemy.

appointed Publius Quinctilius Varus (46 B.C.E.–9 C.E.), a respected senator and friend, to the post of governor of Germania. The power behind the office consisted of three Roman legions, XVII, XVIII, and XIX. These were complemented by three troops of cavalry, called alae, and six cohorts of allied foot soldiers numbering about 3,000 men.

According to the historian Velleius Paterculus (19 B.C.E.–31 C.E.), the reputation of Varus preceded the governor. He had served previously in Gaul and Syria, amassing great wealth. Paterculus, reported to be a political enemy of Varus, asserted that he had come to the rich Roman province of Syria as a poor man and departed a rich man while Syria had been relegated to poverty.

Two years after his appointment, the governor was encamped with his legions west of the Weser River for the summer. In early September, possibly as the legions were relocating to winter quarters near the Rhine, word reached Varus that an insurrection was gaining momentum farther to the west.

TRAITOR OR PATRIOT?

Delivering this alarming news was a trusted advisor, Arminius (17 B.C.E.–21 C.E.). A member of the Cherusci tribe, Arminius had been captured and sent to Rome at the age of 19. During the next five years, he was educated in and acquainted with Roman military tactics. He also became a Roman citizen at the equestrian level, which indicates some measure of personal wealth. Arminius returned to Germania in the year 6 C.E. It is reported that the burdensome taxes levied and harsh

ABOVE: OFTEN FIGHTING IN CLOSE RANKS, Roman legionaries relied on their long spears to keep an enemy at bay. Their short swords were put to use during close combat.

ABOVE: ARMINIUS EXHORTS his Cheruscan tribesmen to destroy the Roman invaders in this nineteenth century etching.

treatment meted out to the Germanic peoples stunned him. Therefore, he turned on his benefactors, reaching out to the chieftains of the independent tribes. At least six of these, the Chatti, Bructeri, Chauci, Sicambri, Marsi, and Cherusci, set aside their differences to strike a blow against the common enemy—Imperial Rome. The plan was simple. The false warning delivered by Arminius himself would arouse Varus

to quell the rebellion. Along the route of march, on ground favorable to the tribal coalition, an ambush would take a heavy toll in Roman lives.

INTO THE UNKNOWN

After setting Varus on an unfamiliar route on September 9, Arminius excused himself, telling the governor that he intended to recruit friendly men to assist the Roman legions. He also asked Varus to divert troops to protect Cherusci settlements from attack. Varus complied with the request

ABOVE: FOLLOWING THE DESTRUCTION OF THREE ROMAN LEGIONS in the Teutoburg Forest, Germanic tribesmen gather numerous trophies from their great victory.

and quickly dismissed what should have been a disturbing revelation from Segestes, a Cheruscan leader who also happened to be the father-in-law of Arminius.

Segestes, who had never approved of his daughter's marriage, warned Varus of the deception and the waiting ambush. The governor, however, chose to press forward. Apparently oblivious to the risk he had assumed, Varus allowed his legions to advance with little attention to military discipline. Women, children, and other camp followers were mingled with the legionaries, and the vulnerable column stretched for miles. Further inviting disaster, Varus failed to send scouting parties ahead of his main line of advance. Violent wind and rain lashed the Romans along their route, which was constricted due to the

thick growth of trees and underbrush. The advance slowed to a crawl as streams were forded or bridged and wagons extricated from the mud. Northeast of present-day Osnabrück in Lower Saxony, Varus entered the dense and hill-studded Teutoburg Forest. The tribesmen knew the terrain well, and it is likely that Arminius and the conspiring chieftains led the vanguard as they fell upon the disorganized Roman column.

THE TRAP IS SPRUNG

Suddenly, the tribesmen leaped to the attack, closing steadily with the enemy. Casualties were horrific, but miraculously some semblance of order was maintained, and the Romans camped in a defensive position on a wooded hillside. The historian Cassius Dio (163?–229? C.E.) recorded that they burned most of their wagons and anything else that was not essential. The following day the Romans

ABOVE: AN UNCOMMON PIECE of battlefield equipment, this face helmet was found near the modern city of Osnabrück, Germany, and is indicative of Germanic craftsmanship.

BELOW RIGHT: THIS HEROIC STATUE OF ARMINIUS, victor of the Battle of the Teutoburg Forest, stands on a hill near the city of Detmold, Germany.

foes, for they had already been wounded, made bold to do a thing that was terrible yet unavoidable. They took their own lives."

AFTERMATH

The deception of Arminius had precipitated the Roman debacle in the Teutoburg Forest, but the ineptitude of Varus had compounded it. Three legions had been wiped out, and their numeric designations would never be used again. Roman prisoners were ransomed, sold into slavery, or sacrificed to pagan gods. The Germanic warriors had suffered few casualties.

During the coming months, Arminius put numerous Roman outposts east of the Rhine to the torch. Seven years of conflict followed, but Germania remained free of Roman domination for the next 400 years. In the end, it was the Roman Empire that declined and fell. To this day, the Battle of the Teutoburg Forest remains a symbol of German nationalism.

forced an opening in the Germanic cordon that had surrounded them. For a time, they were in open country, but soon enough they were deep in the forest once again, their cavalry unable to screen a retreat due to the thick vegetation. Casualties on the second day were even higher than those of the first. Attempting to defend themselves, the legionaries found their swords, javelins, and shields so waterlogged by the torrential rains that they could hardly wield them.

Apparently, Arminius had anticipated the next move by Varus. Slogging through the night, the surviving Romans reached the foot of Kalkriese Hill. Unwittingly, they had marched into a hopeless position. Hemmed in by the heights on one side, an extensive area of marshes on another, and trenches and a large wall of earth thrown up by the tribesmen on a third, the fate of the Romans was sealed. Their tormenters assailed them from the cover of the wall and trenches and from a distance along the flanks.

FUTILE FINAL HOURS

As a desperate attempt to breach the wall ended in failure, the Roman cavalry led by Numonius Vala, second in command to Varus, fled the field, only to be hunted down and slaughtered by Germanic horsemen. Some Roman soldiers suffered the ignominious fate of becoming prisoners. Others, wrote Cassius Dio, chose suicide. "Varus, therefore, and all the more prominent officers, fearing that they should either be captured alive or killed by their bitterest

TEUTOBURG FOREST

2 From camouflaged positions, the Germanic warriors initiate hit-and-run strikes against the extended Roman column and fade into the forest as the Romans deploy.

1 Initially unmolested, the Roman column trudges through heavy forest toward winter quarters. Shadowed by Germanic tribesmen, three legions were soon to be set upon.

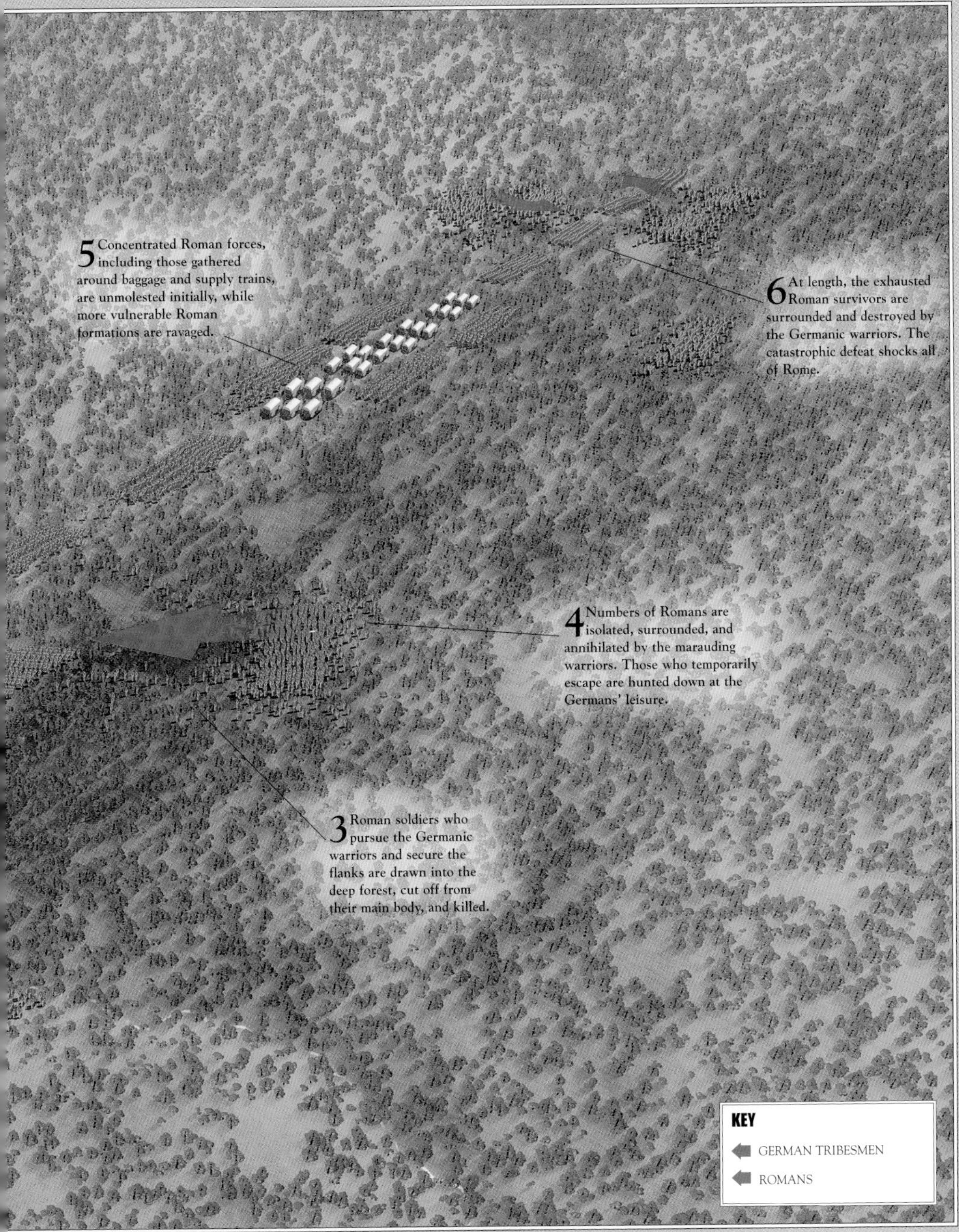

5 Concentrated Roman forces, including those gathered around baggage and supply trains, are unmolested initially, while more vulnerable Roman formations are ravaged.

6 At length, the exhausted Roman survivors are surrounded and destroyed by the Germanic warriors. The catastrophic defeat shocks all of Rome.

4 Numbers of Romans are isolated, surrounded, and annihilated by the marauding warriors. Those who temporarily escape are hunted down at the Germans' leisure.

3 Roman soldiers who pursue the Germanic warriors and secure the flanks are drawn into the deep forest, cut off from their main body, and killed.

KEY

◀ GERMAN TRIBESMEN

◀ ROMANS

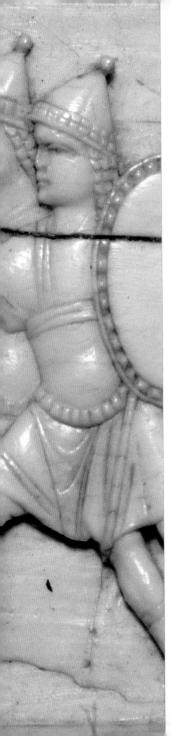

MANZIKERT 1071

The Battle of Manzikert had serious repercussions for the Byzantine Empire, whose strength was never again so great. However, this was due more to the political turmoil that followed defeat than to the battle itself.

The Byzantine Empire (330–1450 C.E.) had its origins in the Eastern Roman Empire. It had enjoyed mixed fortunes but in the middle of the eleventh century Byzantium was a powerful state standing as the protector of Christianity in the West. In 1045, the Empire annexed the city of Ani in Armenia. This was the high-water mark, occurring when the Empire was at its greatest point of expansion. At this time, the Empire stretched all across the Balkans to Dalmatia on the Adriatic Sea coast, as far south as Syria and across Armenia in the east. However, all was not well.

There were significant political problems within the Empire. Factionalism was so bad that the army had begun to depend increasingly on mercenaries, who were less likely to get involved in an assassination or coup attempt than local troops.

MANZIKERT FACTS

Who: A Byzantine army under Emperor Romanus IV Diogenes (ruled 1068–1071), versus a Seljuk army under Sultan Alp Arslan (1029–72).

What: After being worn down in smaller actions the Byzantine army, which fielded 70,000 men at the start of the campaign, was defeated in a pitched battle against the Seljuk army containing 30,000 cavalry.

Where: Near the town of Malazgirt (modern-day Manzikert) in the eastern part of modern Turkey.

When: August 26, 1071 C.E.

Why: The loss of Armenia to the Seljuks required a response, so the Byzantine army marched to retake it.

Outcome: Total defeat for the Byzantines, largely due to a breakdown in command and control.

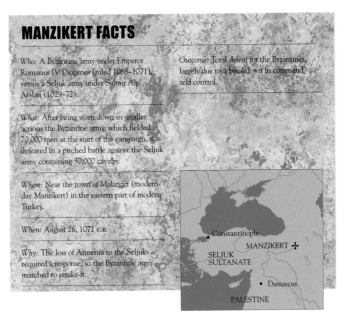

LEFT: *ON THIS TENTH-CENTURY IVORY BOX Byzantine cavalry are depicted fighting with their Turkish adversaries. The Byzantine empire was gradually eroded by peoples from central Asia over a period of centuries.*

ABOVE: ROMANUS IV WAS SENTENCED TO DEATH for his part in a conspiracy to seize the Byzantine throne. He was reprieved and became emperor, only to be deposed after the disaster at Manzikert.

In Armenia there were other problems. The region had previously served as a buffer zone against the nomadic tribes to the east. However, by assuming control, the Byzantines now had to deal with the nomads' raids directly. Many of the Armenian troops who had previously fought the raiders on behalf of the Byzantine Empire had sought employment elsewhere when their princes were conquered, which left the eastern frontier in a weakened position.

ENTER THE SELJUKS

The Seljuks were nomadic horsemen from Central Asia. Migrating westward they encountered the Muslim Caliphate of the Abbasid Dynasty, a great secular and religious state. However, at that time, the state was in political and economic decline. As a result the Seljuks overran the Caliphate and took control by 1054.

With the situation in Armenia very unsettled and the Seljuks established on the border and becoming more and more of a nuisance, Emperor Michael VI (ruled 1056–57) berated his generals for failing to deal with the problem. Rather than serve an ungrateful master, the eastern armies of

Byzantium rebelled and declared their own emperor. Although beaten in battle the rebels staged a successful coup.

Seeing that Byzantium was beset by civil war, the Seljuks began raiding into the Empire in force. Byzantine countermeasures failed badly, not least because the Seljuks' fighting methods were new to their opponents. Seljuk horse archers used a fluid style of warfare that the Byzantine forces could not effectively counter.

In 1064, the Seljuks captured Ani, creating a gap in the line of fortifications that underpinned the Byzantine defensive strategy. Through this gap, raids pushed into the Byzantine heartland. It was obvious that Ani must be retaken or regained by some other means.

BYZANTINE PREPARATIONS

Little had been achieved by 1067, when Emperor Constantine X (born 1006) died, and his wife Eudokia Makrembolitissa (1021–96) was left as regent in the name of her 17-year-old son, Michael Ducas (1050–90). To counter the influence of the Ducas family, Eudokia married Romanus Diogenes (died 1072), a military man with little political power.

The Byzantine army was in a poor state and needed to be reorganized. Units and fortifications had been allowed to decline for generations in an attempt to save money. Romanus undertook a series of rapid reforms intended to offset the

BYZANTINE PELTAST CAVALRYMAN

Heavily armored cataphract cavalry formed the main striking force of the Byzantine army for several centuries. Cataphracts, however, were expensive to raise and maintain. By the time of the Manzikert campaign, the Byzantine Empire had serious financial problems and had been skimping on military funding for decades.

Romanus' army thus made use of lighter cavalry riding unarmored horses and wearing only mail and a helmet. Such lighter forces were more mobile and less affected by heat, but were more vulnerable to enemy action, especially missile fire, which could bring down horses.

ABOVE: A FIFTEENTH-CENTURY depiction of the Battle of Manzikert shows the combatants in Western European armor of a much later period. Emperor Romanus makes his escape by horse in the foreground.

worst of the problems and in 1068–69 went on campaign in Syria and Armenia. The Seljuk horse archers remained out of Romanus' reach but the campaigns did provide some useful operational experience. Political troubles hamstrung Romanus' attempts to campaign against the Seljuks for the next year, 1070, and he decided that decisive action was needed. A victory over the Seljuks would both deal with that problem and rally support to his own cause. It seemed to Romanus that this was a reasonable gamble, so in 1071 he began preparations for a campaign.

THE CAMPAIGN

Romanus set out from Constantinople at the head of a sizable force. His army contained mercenaries from various parts of Europe as well as professional troops from the Empire and local forces raised for the campaign or bribed into service along the way. The quality of these troops varied but

this was not Romanus' main problem. Members of the Ducas faction held key posts in the army and their loyalty was highly suspect.

Romanus advanced into Armenia in the hope of forcing a battle with the Seljuks. However, he was able to obtain little information about their forces, while the Seljuk Sultan Alp Arslan was informed of Romanus' doings on a regular basis. Abandoning his own campaign against Aleppo, Arslan marched to meet Romanus. This was not without problems; troops willing to serve against Aleppo in the hope of plunder were not so keen to fight in Armenia and melted away. However, Arslan was able to obtain more men, finally reaching Armenia in August with about 30,000 cavalry.

Romanus unwisely divided his forces, and Byzantine politics now took a hand. A detachment numbering about half the total Byzantine army encountered a strong Seljuk force and withdrew rather than fight. The detachment then turned around and marched home to Constantinople without informing Romanus of the encounter.

SELJUK HORSE ARCHER

Like many Asiatic people, the Seljuks used light cavalry armed with bows as their arm of decision. Horse archers were available only to nomadic cultures because it took many years for a man to become competent in shooting from the saddle while retaining control of his mount. As a result, the Europeans had little experience of their mode of combat, and had trouble countering it.

Horse archers could bring their firepower to bear rapidly at any point on the battlefield and make a swift strategic redeployment. They could function as scouts as well as missile troops, and if the situation merited it they could also charge in with scimitar and buckler, combining their harassing fire with shock action.

THE BATTLE OF MANZIKERT

On August 24, 1071, Romanus' main force and that of his Seljuk enemies met for the first time. The Byzantines were not concentrated, allowing the Seljuks to gain a significant advantage. A force under Nicephorus Bryennius came under attack but managed to extricate itself by hard fighting. However, a relief force sent to Bryennius' assistance was ambushed and roughly handled.

Romanus reorganized his army on August 25, ready to fight a more coordinated action the next day, and on August 26 he marched out to give battle. In the center were the elite Varangian Guard under Romanus' personal command, backed up by mercenary troops. Other infantry were deployed to either side of the Varangians, with light cavalry on the flanks. A reserve force was assembled behind the line. The choice of Andronicus Ducas as commander of the reserve was to prove disastrous.

As the Byzantines began to advance, the Seljuk force used classic horse-archer tactics, which involved shooting and then withdrawing to prevent a decisive contact. The Byzantine light cavalry became involved in a skirmish with some of the Seljuks but were not able to pin the main force.

Romanus' army pressed forward with resolution and managed to capture the Seljuk camp. This was often seen as an indicator of victory, but the Seljuks maintained the pressure and eventually Romanus was forced to fall back.

COLLAPSE AND BETRAYAL

The Byzantine right wing, consisting mainly of Armenian troops, had been under heavy fire all day. As the order was passed to begin a retirement, the wing became badly disordered and some units broke up. The panic spread and soon much of the right wing was in rout.

The Seljuks closed in for the kill, and Romanus' only real hope for escape lay in a swift intervention by his reserve. However, its commander was a rival whose interests were best served by leaving Romanus to his fate. The reserve simply withdrew, triggering the collapse of morale in some units.

The left wing of the Byzantine army was able to fight its way free and escape, but the center force remained trapped. Romanus' bodyguard of Varangians and a large force of mercenaries remained loyal, but they suffered very heavy losses before surrendering.

OUTCOMES

Romanus was freed by his Seljuk captors in return for a large ransom, but returned home to face a coup. A short period of civil war ensued until Romanus surrendered and was savagely treated by the Ducas clan.

ABOVE: *A MEDIEVAL DEPICTION of the Varangian Guard at Constantinople. The Varangians were famed for their use of the two-handed axe, but some may have fought mounted with sword or lance.*

LEFT: *A THIRTEENTH-CENTURY RELIEF of Seljuk warriors. Their armor is lamellar, an alternative to mail formed of short strips of metal fastened together rather than to an undergarment of padding or leather.*

This did not end the troubles in Byzantium. In fact, it sparked a downward spiral of internal conflict and raiding by various neighboring tribes that continually destabilized the Byzantine state. The Empire survived but the aftermath of Manzikert, rather than the battle itself, was the beginning of its final decline.

Romanus' defeat at Manzikert is attributable to two main causes. Many years of neglect had caused the decline of the Byzantine army and greatly reduced its fighting efficiency. But it was politics that doomed the Byzantines at Manzikert. Lack of trust among commanders contributed to the desertion of a large part of the army before and during the battle, and Ducas' deliberate betrayal was, of course, politically motivated.

MANZIKERT

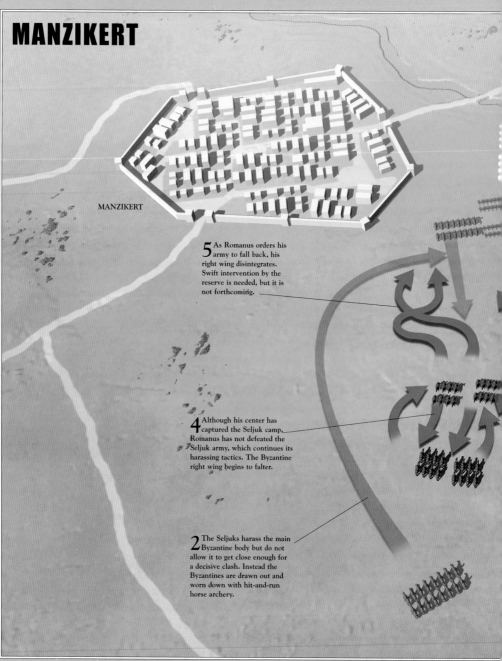

MANZIKERT

5 As Romanus orders his army to fall back, his right wing disintegrates. Swift intervention by the reserve is needed, but it is not forthcoming.

4 Although his center has captured the Seljuk camp, Romanus has not defeated the Seljuk army, which continues its harassing tactics. The Byzantine right wing begins to falter.

2 The Seljuks harass the main Byzantine body but do not allow it to get close enough for a decisive clash. Instead the Byzantines are drawn out and worn down with hit-and-run horse archery.

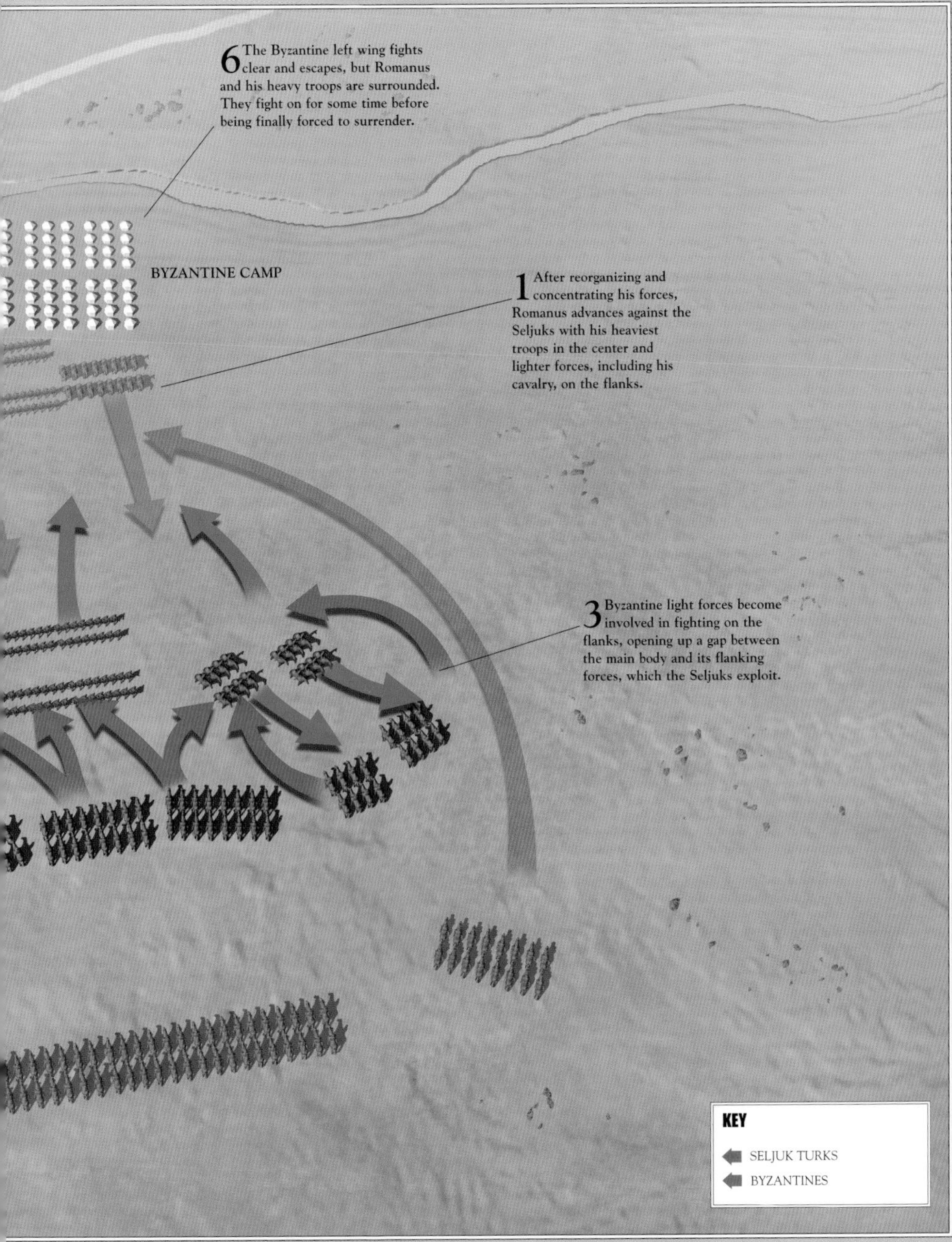

6 The Byzantine left wing fights clear and escapes, but Romanus and his heavy troops are surrounded. They fight on for some time before being finally forced to surrender.

BYZANTINE CAMP

1 After reorganizing and concentrating his forces, Romanus advances against the Seljuks with his heaviest troops in the center and lighter forces, including his cavalry, on the flanks.

3 Byzantine light forces become involved in fighting on the flanks, opening up a gap between the main body and its flanking forces, which the Seljuks exploit.

KEY

SELJUK TURKS

BYZANTINES

HATTIN 1187

In the wake of the Second Crusade, a powerful Saracen leader emerged, unifying Egypt and Syria and surrounding the Crusader Kingdom on the eastern rim of the Mediterranean Sea. Saladin, the Sultan of Egypt, maintained an uneasy truce with the Christians who occupied Jerusalem.

However, while a tenuous external peace held, infighting, political intrigue, and the quest for fortune had fostered fractious internal relationships. The religious zeal that characterized the initial crusade urged by Pope Urban II (1042–99) nearly a century earlier, to wrest territories of the Holy Land from Muslim rule, had been tempered by more worldly pursuits. Amid turmoil, Guy of Lusignan (1150–94) was crowned King of Jerusalem in 1186, nearly igniting a war with Raymond III of Tripoli (1140–87), regent to King Baldwin V (1177–86), who had died earlier that year at the age of nine.

While at odds with the new king, Raymond concluded a separate treaty with Saladin and refused to recognize the sovereign. Meanwhile, Guy was capable of exercising only limited authority over the barons and nobles who had journeyed

HATTIN FACTS

Who: Christian forces under King Guy versus the Saracen army of Saladin, Sultan of Egypt (1138–93).

What: The Christian army, harassed by the mobile Saracens and ineptly led by King Guy, was decimated.

Where: The Horns of Hattin, near Tiberias, in present-day Israel.

When: July 4, 1187.

Why: The Christian army marched with intent to relieve the besieged fortress of Tiberias.

Outcome: The army of King Guy suffered terribly and was completely destroyed by the Saracens. Saladin was able to capture the Crusader port of Acre, cutting off the Christian Kingdom of Jerusalem from the sea. In September Saladin laid siege to Jerusalem, and by October 2 had captured the Holy City.

LEFT: *THE DEFEATED CRUSADERS offer their arms after the catastrophic defeat at Hattin. The defeat prompted the launch of the Third Crusade, which recaptured Acre in 1191.*

eastward with the Second Crusade, and conflict with Saladin and the Muslims was an inevitable byproduct. The consequences of the looming showdown at Hattin would reverberate across the known world.

A PRINCELY PROVOCATION

When the Second Crusade ended in 1149, one adventurer who remained in the East was Reynald of Chatillon (1125–87). Proclaimed Lord of Oultrejourdain, southeast of Jerusalem, Reynald regularly attacked Muslim trade caravans, violating treaties and agreements of safe passage.

CRUSADER KNIGHT

His tunic and shield emblazoned with the Cross, this crusader knight is armed with a long sword. His outer garment covers a suit of chain mail from head to toe. An extension of the bowl-shaped helmet offers minimal protection to the nose and face. Armor, however, proved to be a hindrance in the arid climate of the Middle Eastern desert.

ABOVE: IN THIS FRENCH PAINTING, entitled "The Miracle of the True Cross," reflects the Crusaders' belief that they marched with the Cross upon which Jesus died.

Late in 1186, Reynald struck once more, seizing a large caravan traveling north across his fiefdom from Cairo, holding the merchants for ransom, and slaughtering the guard. Saladin, whose own territorial ambitions had met with initial success but had been brought to an end in defeat at the Battle of Montgisard in 1177, demanded that Reynald return the seized goods and free the hostages. This plea fell upon deaf ears. Saladin then appealed directly to King Guy, who instructed Reynald to surrender his ill-gotten booty. When Reynald again refused, it became apparent that war would come.

TREATY AND TRIBULATION

Raymond's treaty with Saladin came back to haunt him. While Guy assembled the forces of his confederation, attempting to march into nearby Galilee and defeat Saladin swiftly, a force of 6,500 Saracens commanded by Saladin's son, Al-Afdal (1160–96), advanced into the Kingdom of Jerusalem, receiving permission to cross Raymond's lands in accordance with the terms of the treaty.

In the path of Al-Afdal's advance with 7,000 cavalry lay a small force of 140 Knights Templar and Knights Hospitaller and 350 infantrymen. Although their intended purpose had been to end the dispute between Raymond and Guy, the Grand Masters of these Orders were spoiling for a fight and impetuously attacked the larger Saracen force. Only three members of the Templar contingent survived. Ironically, in death these poorly led soldiers had accomplished their original mission. The schism between Guy and Raymond, who blamed himself for the catastrophe, was healed.

Saladin, however, had made good use of time, raising an army of more than 20,000 infantrymen and 10,000 cavalry. Recognizing the threat from without, the Christians in peril had managed to marshal a defensive force of 20,000, which included 1,200 knights and 15,000 infantrymen.

THE OPPOSING FORCES

At first glance, the opposing Christian and Muslim forces appeared to be reasonably matched, but on the eve of the decisive Battle of Hattin, the armies were of a very different character. The forces of Saladin consisted of light infantry armed with spears, shields, and the formidable bow and arrow. The cavalry, armed with bow and lance, were mainly Askari,

ABOVE: *AFTER KILLING A CHRISTIAN DURING THE CRUSADES, Saladin, Sultan of Egypt and Syria, raises his hands in exultation.*

MEN-AT-ARMS

Serving as the infantry of the Crusader forces, men-at-arms were often armed with spears, battleaxes, or slow-firing crossbows. Wearing suits of chain mail or padded outer garments along with large helmets, they were often less mobile than their Saracen counterparts. By the time of the Battle of Hattin, a lengthy march had eroded the combat effectiveness of these foot soldiers.

skilled horsemen from Syria and Egypt. In contrast, the Christian forces consisted of heavily armored, mounted knights, infantry armed with spears and slow-firing crossbows, and a small complement of Turcopoles, mounted-archer mercenaries whose services had been financed by King Henry II of England. While the knights themselves were superb shock troops—given the proper circumstances—the Christian force lacked its adversary's speed and mobility.

ADVANCE TO OBLIVION

Rather than attacking the Christians directly, Saladin sacked the village of Tiberias and laid siege to the nearby fortress, hoping to draw Guy out to fight in the open. Raymond, whose own wife, Eschiva (1159–87), was temporarily safe inside the walls at Tiberias, urged caution. Reinforcements were expected from Antioch, while water and food were plentiful at Acre.

Nevertheless, Guy felt obliged to march to the relief of besieged Tiberias. Failing to grasp the implications of his decision, the king ordered his army forward. On the night of July 2, 1187, the Christian force camped at Sephoria, near a good source of water. While Raymond continued to plead for restraint, others, including Reynald of Chatillon, agitated for a continuing advance.

Guy knew that an army of heavily armored soldiers and their hundreds of horses could not possibly traverse the Plain of Toran, where there was no water, then approach Tiberias directly and take on the Saracens without having their fighting efficiency seriously degraded. Ignoring Raymond, he chose a calculated risk. The army was to proceed to Tiberias across the Wadi Hamman, where a source of water was supposed to be found.

On the morning of July 3, the Christian force renewed its advance, playing into Saladin's hands. Marching six miles (10 km) in the swelter, and continually harassed by bands of Saladin's swift archers, they paused at Turan and drank their last from a nearby spring. They were still nearly 10 miles (16 km) from Tiberias in the blazing afternoon sun. It would have made sense for the army to halt for the night. However, Guy committed yet another blunder and ordered his parched army to continue. As the Christians neared the Horns of Hattin, a double hill formation within sight of the Sea of Galilee, Saladin sent a strong force sweeping behind Guy to seize the spring at Turan and cut off Guy's escape route. Rather than fully engaging, the Saracens stood off and rained arrows on their hapless enemy. Guy halted on the high ground. During the night, Saladin's soldiers lit fires, and the choking smoke compounded the misery of the Christians.

TIGHTENING THE NOOSE

As the sun rose on July 4, a panic gripped the Crusader infantry, which broke in a desperate effort to reach the Sea of Galilee. Hemmed in by Saladin's troops, they were forced onto the eastern horn. Those who were not killed were taken prisoner. With its infantry screen decimated, the knights had little choice but to attack. If they remained stationary, their horses would be easy marks for Muslim bows.

Raymond gallantly led about 200 knights in a bold charge, hoping to break out of the cordon, but the mobile Saracens merely flexed and allowed the heavy Christian cavalry to shoot its bolt. Wounded three times, Raymond managed to escape with a few of his number. The majority of the knights, however, were trapped on the western horn. Three more desperate charges proved futile, and the dwindling force collapsed around the tent of King Guy.

BELOW: ASTRIDE SWIFT ARABIAN MOUNTS, the Egyptian Mameluk cavalrymen of Saladin's Muslim army were lightly armored and carried long lances, which were effective against massed infantry.

At last, the exhausted defenders capitulated. Among Saladin's prisoners were several other nobles, Reynald, and Guy himself. About 200 Knights Templar and Hospitaller, sworn enemies of the Saracens, were beheaded swiftly. Saladin was said to have executed Reynald personally. Estimates of the Christian casualties are as high as 17,000. King Guy was eventually ransomed and set free.

After his decisive victory at Hattin, Saladin quickly captured Acre and several other cities. Jerusalem fell on October 2, and news of these dramatic reversals shocked all of Christendom.

RIGHT: NEAR TIBERIAS IN PRESENT-DAY ISRAEL, the battlefield of Hattin looks much as it did when it was the scene of the disastrous defeat of the Crusaders at the hands of Saladin in 1187.

BELOW: THE BODIES OF DEAD CRUSADERS, pierced repeatedly by Muslim arrows, lie in a heap with a crucifix among them. A dove and circle of stars, depicting the Holy Spirit, hover above.

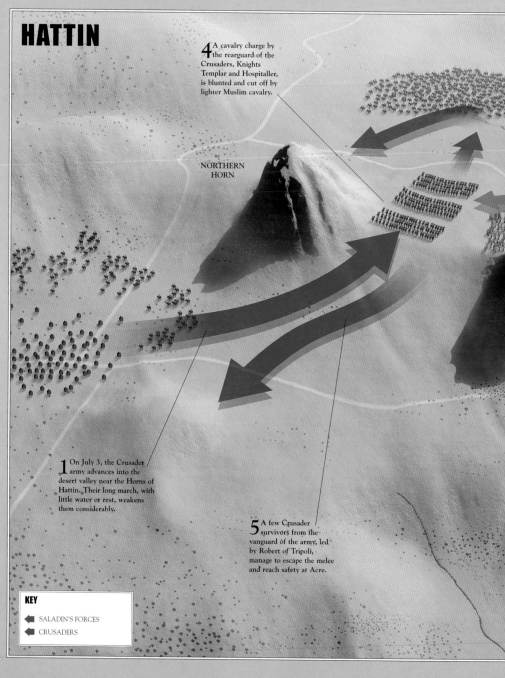

HATTIN

4 A cavalry charge by the rearguard of the Crusaders, Knights Templar and Hospitaller, is blunted and cut off by lighter Muslim cavalry.

NORTHERN
HORN

1 On July 3, the Crusader army advances into the desert valley near the Horns of Hattin. Their long march, with little water or rest, weakens them considerably.

5 A few Crusader survivors from the vanguard of the army, led by Robert of Tripoli, manage to escape the melee and reach safety at Acre.

KEY

SALADIN'S FORCES

CRUSADERS

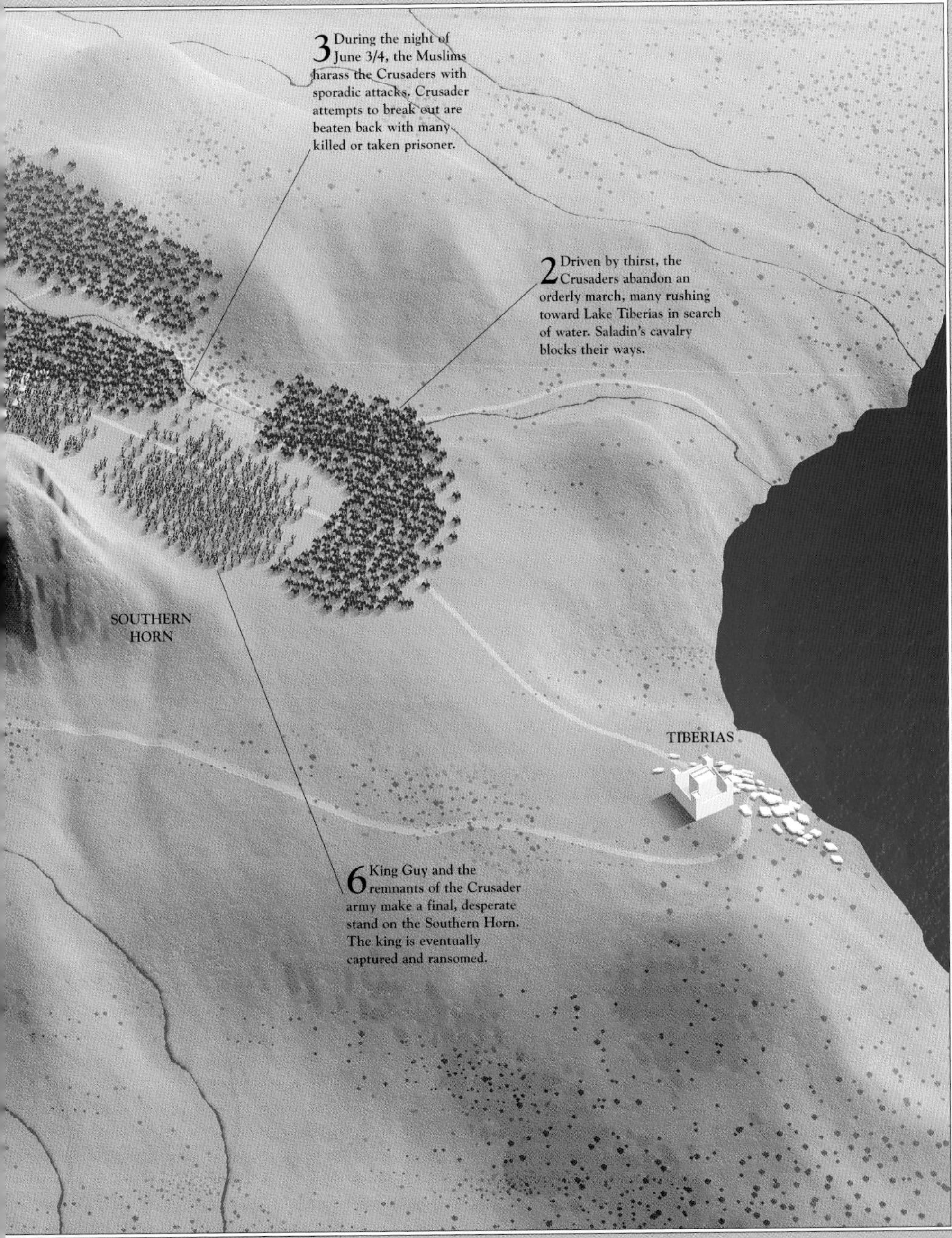

3 During the night of June 3/4, the Muslims harass the Crusaders with sporadic attacks. Crusader attempts to break out are beaten back with many killed or taken prisoner.

2 Driven by thirst, the Crusaders abandon an orderly march, many rushing toward Lake Tiberias in search of water. Saladin's cavalry blocks their ways.

SOUTHERN HORN

TIBERIAS

6 King Guy and the remnants of the Crusader army make a final, desperate stand on the Southern Horn. The king is eventually captured and ransomed.

AGINCOURT 1415

The Hundred Years' War was in its eighth decade when King Henry V defeated the French at the Battle of Agincourt. The great conflict had arisen at various times due to English claims to the throne of France, French interference in England's wars with Scotland, and English trade and economic power in continental Europe, particularly in French-dominated Flanders.

In the summer of 1415, Henry V (1388–1422) and an army of 12,000 set sail for France. His motive was three-fold. Henry intended to assert his claim to lands in Normandy, which he believed had been unjustly confiscated by Charles VI, king of France (1368–1422). The prosecution of a successful war against a traditional enemy would enhance the prestige of the young king, who was not yet 30, and, finally, it was the custom of the day to ransom captured noblemen who had been taken on the field of battle. These payments would line Henry's coffers.

AGINCOURT FACTS

Who: The English army under King Henry V versus the French army commanded by Charles d'Albret, Constable of France

What: The small English army—fewer than 6,000 men— utilizing the longbow and the advantages offered by the terrain, thoroughly defeated a much larger French force of 20,000–30,000 men.

Where: Near the village of Agincourt in northern France.

When: October 25, 1415.

Why: King Henry V asserted claims to territory in France and sought greater prestige at home.

Outcome: The greatest English victory of the Hundred Years' War, Agincourt was a devastating defeat for France.

ENGLAND
London •

✛ AGINCOURT

Paris •

FRANCE

LEFT: IN THIS FIFTEENTH-CENTURY REPRESENTATION of the Battle of Agincourt, heavily armored French knights fall victim to English infantry, cavalry, and longbowmen.

campaigning had taken their toll when a colossal French force finally confronted them in a narrow field flanked on each side by heavy forest near the village of Agincourt. Ahead, was a host of the enemy commanded by Charles d'Albret (1369–1415), Count of Dreux, Constable of France.

MEN-AT-ARMS

Accounts vary as to the relative strength of the combatants at Agincourt. However, the English are thought to have dwindled to less than 6,000 while estimates of French strength

ENGLISH LONGBOWMAN

The effective use of the longbow gave the English army the decisive advantage against French knights at Agincourt. A skilled longbowman was typically capable of discharging up to six arrows per minute. He wore the gambeson—cushioned to absorb the blows of enemy weapons—during combat and carried a short dagger for defense.

ABOVE: KING HENRY V was not yet 30 when he embarked on his campaign in France. William Shakespeare immortalized the Agincourt victory.

A significant measure of risk accompanied the English foray into France. Henry's forces would be campaigning in hostile territory, and they numbered a relative few. The reward, he reasoned, was worth the great gamble.

SIEGE AND SUFFERING

After landing on the continent on August 13, 1415, the English besieged the port city of Harfleur (Le Havre), which fell on September 22. Although victorious, the siege had cost Henry hundreds of casualties, primarily due to rampaging dysentery. As autumn weather signaled the end of the year's campaigning, the English headed for the port of Calais to rest during the winter. While Henry prosecuted his siege at Harfleur, the French raised a formidable army that paralleled the invaders as they trekked northward and sought a suitable crossing of the Somme River.

Initial attempts to cross the Somme were blocked by the French, but the English countermarched southward, made a crossing, and then turned once again, northward toward succor at Calais and the might of their enemy. The English had begun their march from Harfleur on October 8, and months of

ABOVE: IN THIS PAINTING *based on Shakespeare's play Henry V, the English pray prior to going into battle at Agincourt.*

vary widely, with their true number probably somewhere between 20,000 and 30,000.

The English army consisted of approximately 900 men-at-arms and 5,000 archers employing the famed longbow. The French force included at least some 8,000 men-at-arms, 5,500 archers and crossbowmen, and possibly more than 6,000 mounted knights. Men-at-arms were professional soldiers of somewhat higher social standing than the archers but lower than the knights. They were typically armed with swords and fought either mounted or on foot. Members of the nobility,

considered by both sides to be potential prizes of battle, might be exchanged for ransom. The common fighters, however, struggled under no such illusions. If captured, they could expect to be disposed of swiftly.

On the eve of battle, the English spent another miserable night exposed to a heavy rain. The French, confident of victory against the puny English, dined sumptuously and eagerly awaited daybreak.

TERRIBLE TERRAIN

One great advantage for the English at Agincourt was the ground on which the battle would be fought. The narrow confines of the field itself would naturally neutralize the

French numerical superiority, funneling the Constable's forces into a tight front. Perhaps worse for the French, a week of torrential rain had turned the freshly plowed field into a quagmire. Horses' hooves and heavily armored knights could not maneuver effectively in mud that was often ankle deep.

DAY OF DECISION

On the morning of Friday, October 25, 1415, St. Crispin's Day, King Henry V arrayed his army across 750 yards (685 m) of soggy earth, probably with archers on either flank, men-at-arms and knights in the center supported by a small contingent of archers. The foot soldiers stood in ranks four deep, while the archers sharpened stakes, called palings, which would then be driven into the ground in front of them as protection against an enemy cavalry charge. With the king in overall command, Edward of Norwich, the Duke of York (1373–1415) directed the English on the right, and Thomas, Lord Camoys (?–1421) commanded the left. Should the British line falter, there could be no retreat, and no reserves were available. The French were deployed in lines called battles. As many as three of these formations

BELOW: THE FIFTEENTH-CENTURY FRENCH KNIGHT was well-armed with a variety of swords and sidearms and heavily protected by armor, but this limited his mobility on foot.

ABOVE: THIS NINETEENTH-CENTURY illustration of the fighting depicts a wild melee between mounted French and English knights.

participated in the fight. They included 4,000 archers, 8,000 men-at-arms, and supporting crossbowmen. Ranks of cavalry were positioned on both flanks. Jean le Meingre Boucicaut (1366–1421), Marshal of France, and Constable d'Albret led the first French line, while Prince Charles d'Artois (dates unknown) and John I, Duke of Alençon (1385–1415) commanded the second.

THE EPIC CLASH

Expecting more reinforcements, the French did not initiate combat. Henry realized that time was not his ally, but the two sides watched each other warily for several hours. Finally, Henry ordered his archers to pull their palings from the ground and advance to within 300 yards (275 m) of the French lines, where they began the fighting with a cloud of arrows.

Henry's bold move thwarted the French plan to attack with cavalry once their archers had shaken the English, but the archers had been shunted toward the rear of the French formations and were not in position to deliver their volley of missiles. Nevertheless, the French cavalry came forward, impeded by their own ranks of dismounted men-at-arms and the muddy terrain. Once in the open, the cavalrymen found they could not flank the English longbowmen, because of the heavy woods or assault them directly, because of the palings. The attack disintegrated, and panicked horses, their riders fallen in the muck, trampled men and threw formations into confusion.

Next came the dismounted men-at-arms, with the Constable at their head. As they slogged through the mud, weighed down by their heavy armor, the longbowmen put up a withering curtain of fire. The bodies of dead and wounded Frenchmen impeded their progress further, and those who lost their footing were easy prey for the English. When their supply of arrows was exhausted the English archers dropped their bows, picked up whatever was at hand, and waded into the foundering French. So closely packed were the Frenchmen that many could not effectively wield their weapons. The second French line was committed to the fray and suffered a similar fate.

During the three-hour brawl, the French lost as many as 10,000 killed and some 1,500 noblemen captured, while the English suffered fewer than 500 casualties, including just more than 100 dead. Clearly

the French had exercised poor judgment in delaying their attack against an inferior force, allowing the enemy to dictate the course of the battle, and failing to consider the nature of the terrain. The result was humiliating defeat.

POSTSCRIPT

Although his army had won a resounding victory, Henry was informed that a small French force had pillaged the baggage train in his rear. Fearing a renewed attack by the French, he ordered the slaughter of all prisoners to prevent them from rearming. The nobles, who could be ransomed, were spared. The executions proved unnecessary.

Agincourt sounded the death knell of the chivalrous knight and displayed the value of the longbow, the artillery of the day. Henry and his small army, having prevailed against long odds, returned to England in triumph.

BELOW: A NINETEENTH-CENTURY WATERCOLOR PAINTING of Agincourt shows French knights falling before the concentrated barrage of English arrows as King Henry V observes.

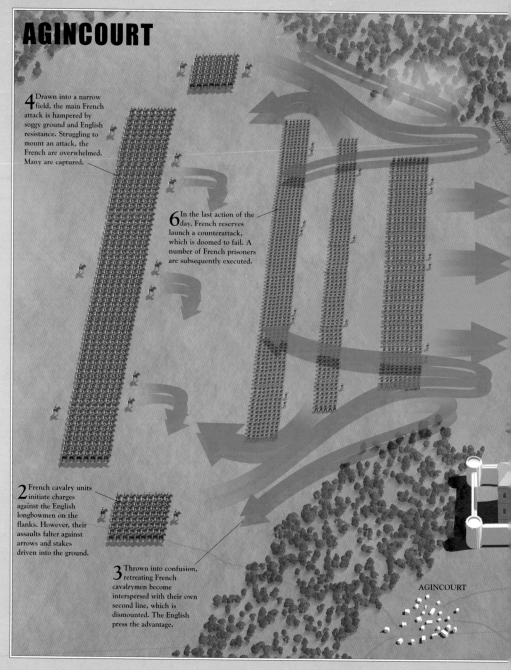

AGINCOURT

4 Drawn into a narrow field, the main French attack is hampered by soggy ground and English resistance. Struggling to mount an attack, the French are overwhelmed. Many are captured.

6 In the last action of the day, French reserves launch a counterattack, which is doomed to fail. A number of French prisoners are subsequently executed.

2 French cavalry units initiate charges against the English longbowmen on the flanks. However, their assaults falter against arrows and stakes driven into the ground.

3 Thrown into confusion, retreating French cavalrymen become interspersed with their own second line, which is dismounted. The English press the advantage.

AGINCOURT

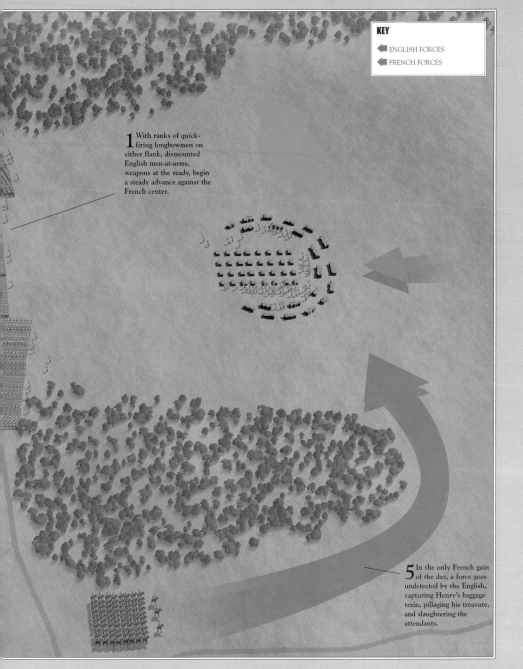

KEY

◀ ENGLISH FORCES

◀ FRENCH FORCES

1 With ranks of quick-firing longbowmen on either flank, dismounted English men-at-arms, weapons at the ready, begin a steady advance against the French center.

5 In the only French gain of the day, a force goes undetected by the English, capturing Henry's baggage train, pillaging his treasure, and slaughtering the attendants.

LEPANTO

1571

Before the Battle of Lepanto the Turkish fleet seemed all but unbeatable. However, recent developments in armament, along with the tactics to go with them, permitted the Holy League to defeat a superior force of Turkish galleys.

The Ottoman Turks were immensely powerful in the middle of the sixteenth century, and conflict with European powers was common. Europe was at the time weak and divided by internal conflicts, which made it possible for the Turks to push steadily into European territory, at one point besieging Vienna. Meanwhile the powerful Ottoman fleet attacked the ships and holdings of maritime states, such as Venice and Genoa.

Galleys were used for both commerce and war in the Mediterranean, and Ottoman tactics were built around the use of their galleys as archery platforms, with the ability to ram and sink an enemy vessel a useful way to deliver a decisive blow. This mode of naval warfare was becoming obsolete as new weapons became available, but this had not yet become apparent. Up until the Battle of Lepanto, Ottoman skill

LEPANTO FACTS

Who: An Ottoman Turk fleet containing around 275 ships opposed by 206 galleys and six galleasses of the Christian Holy League.

Outcome: Decisive defeat of the Turkish Ottoman fleet, who suffered most of their ships either sunk or captured.

What: The massed fleets met in a set-piece galley battle.

Where: Off the coast at Lepanto at the northern edge of the Gulf of Patras off western Greece.

When: October 7, 1571.

Why: The Holy League was formed to halt Ottoman Turkish expansion in the Mediterranean.

Constantinople •

LEPANTO ✛

OTTOMAN EMPIRE

Mediterranean Sea

LEFT: THE BATTLE OF LEPANTO. *A distinguishing feature of the great decisive naval battles in history has been the willingness of both sides to fight the issue out to a final and conclusive finish.*

ABOVE: POPE PIUS V formed the Holy League to protect Christian holdings against Ottoman expansion in the Mediterranean.

JANISSARY ARCHER

Taken and converted, the original janissaries began life as Christian boys levied from the Ottoman Empire's Slavic territories. Kept celibate and strictly Muslim by Turkish officers, they constituted the elite of the Ottoman army and its most feared combat arm. This archer carries the dreaded and effective short composite bow, which was made famous in cavalry action but was equally handy and lethal in the crowded confines of combat at sea. His distinctive headgear identified his type and reputation to his opponents, while offering some measure of protection. The Turkish short bow was made of laminated wood and horn, which were held together by a glue that suffered from long exposure to moisture. Its range and power, if not its accuracy or rate of fire, was comparable to the English longbow. Christian armor and arquebuses proved an effective counter.

and tactics always overwhelmed enemies who tried to fight on the same terms. This might have gone on had the Europeans not changed the way they fought.

The European states were moving away from archery in favor of gunpowder weapons. The arquebuses (muzzle-loaded firearms) of the time were not superior to bows by any means. They were less accurate, had a shorter range, and could not drop fire over an obstruction the way archers could. However, it was relatively quick and simple to train a professional arquebusier, and the heavy ball had a powerful impact.

The real key to European superiority was the cannon. The Ottoman fleet carried guns, of course, but these were smaller, lighter, and less efficient on average than the European

RIGHT: A FLOATING FORTRESS, the galleass was the ultimate and unwieldy result of an effort to combine both oars and broadside, taxing human muscle to the limit. Heavy cannon and high bulwarks made them dangerous attackers—and also impossible targets. If they could not run down an enemy, they had little need to run away from one.

versions. More importantly perhaps, they were not rated highly by the Ottoman commanders and thus not given the chance to perform to their utmost. There were also far fewer of them—750 to the Europeans' 1,800.

Among the European forces were six galleasses, large merchant galleys converted to carry powerful batteries of cannon along the sides and in raised "castles" fore and aft. European cannon were better than those of their opponents, but this advantage would be important only if the tactics in use permitted it.

FORMATION OF THE HOLY LEAGUE

Pope Pius V (1504–72) called for the creation of an alliance to prevent further Ottoman incursions and to protect Cyprus, then a Venetian holding, from attack. The alliance took time to form, and before its forces were ready the Ottoman Sultan,

BELOW: A PAINTING OF THE BATTLE OF LEPANTO by J.H. Valda illustrates the bitter close-quarters fighting of a boarding action amid the smoke of muskets and cannon.

Selim II (1524–74), ordered his fleet to move on Cyprus. On July 3, 1570 the Ottoman fleet, under Ali Pasha (died 1571), landed a large force on the island and immediately moved west to prevent a relief force from interfering in the conquest. Ali Pasha had started his career as a soldier on land and was still more a landsman than an admiral. Nevertheless he commanded a powerful force, which had not seen a major defeat in two centuries, and was sailing under the holy Banner of the Caliphs. All that had gone before justified his confidence.

Meanwhile, the Holy League was assembling its forces. In overall command was Don Juan of Austria (1547–78). The bulk of the fleet came from Venice, comprising 109 galleys and 6 galleasses. The second-largest contingent was made up of 80 galleys from Spain. The remainder of the fleet was made up of small contributions from Malta, Savoy, Genoa, the Papal States, and a handful of private individuals.

Once assembled, the Christian fleet sailed eastward toward Cyprus. Naturally, Ali Pasha came out to intercept the

move. On October 7, 1571, 210 Christian vessels faced 275 Ottoman galleys off the coast of Greece.

THE BATTLE BEGINS

Both sides formed up in four bodies consisting of a center, two wings, and a reserve force. The Christians pushed their galleasses out in front of the main body while the Ottomans advanced confidently, keen to get into bow range and begin winning the battle. The Christian right wing was somewhat out of position at this point, mainly due to having the greatest distance to travel when rounding Point Scropha on the Greek coast.

As the Ottoman force advanced, the galleasses opened fire with their cannon, which came as something of a shock. The galleasses were converted merchant vessels and did not look like conventional warships; they had been mistaken for supply vessels.

LEFT: MARCANTONIO COLONNA was one of the commanders of the Christian central division. After the battle he was named admiral of the Papal fleet.

BELOW: THE TRADITIONAL MODE OF GALLEY WARFARE, as shown here, was a close-quarters brawl of boarding actions and point-blank shooting. The Christians' heavy cannon gave them a range and firepower advantage.

Two Ottoman galleys were sunk and others damaged, with significant disruption to the battle formation, before the Ottoman force closed to bow range.

The Ottoman galleys were adeptly and boldly handled, advancing in a broad crescent to engage their opposite numbers. Commanders of groups and individual ships seized opportunities that presented themselves. The commander of the southern division, Uluj Ali (1519–87), saw the Christian right wing shifting southward to avoid being flanked. This increased an already sizable gap in the Christian line between the right and center divisions. Uluj Ali then switched his force northward, hitting the flank of the main Christian division and creating a local superiority while the 53 galleys of the Christian right wing were out of position.

The 62 galleys of the Christian center were hard pressed. The force in front of them had a similar number of galleys plus 32 lighter galiots (small galleys with one or two masts and 20 oars), and the flanking group was also powerful. However, the 30 galleys of the Christian central reserve and the Christian right wing, coming into action at last, stabilized the situation, and a pounding match ensued.

Meanwhile, the Christian left wing, near the shore, was suffering as well. A fast force of Ottoman galleys made a flanking move and for a time the line was threatened. Gradually, however, the situation was brought under control. The cannon of the galleasses were instrumental in this. They were heavy enough to smash and sink ships, and the weight of fire began to tell.

THE CANNON TRIUMPHS

The Battle of Lepanto had much in common with a land battle in many ways, with enemy units softened up by missile fire and finished off by shock action in the form of boarding parties. Several vessels on either side were boarded and captured, sometimes changing hands more than once.

However, the cannon of the Christian ships proved decisive. Ottoman vessels closing to board had great holes blown in them, killing many men and often preventing a successful attack. At bow range, cannon could not miss and did far more damage than arrows could. The Ottoman guns—never considered a decisive weapon—were insufficiently supplied and ran out of ammunition.

The cannon tipped the balance, especially where the galleasses could pound other ships into flinders from a distance. However, there were more traditional elements to the Ottoman defeat. Ali Pasha was hit in the head by a musket ball and his vessel successfully boarded. Displaying his head on a pike and in possession of the Banner of the Caliphs, the Christians demoralized their foes and forced them into retreat.

As the tide turned, most of the Ottoman fleet was captured or sunk. In all, the Ottomans lost about as many ships as the Christians started with. Uluj Ali was able to

ABOVE: THE BATTLE OF LEPANTO was instantly recognized as a significant victory, inspiring paintings by contemporary artists, such as Venetian Paolo Veronese (1528–88).

break off action and retreat with much of his force, but annihilation was more or less complete for the remainder of the Ottoman fleet.

OUTCOMES

The immediate effect of the battle of Lepanto was to greatly reduce Turkish naval power in the Mediterranean, which also brought about a reduction in the amount of corsair activity in the area. However, the Holy League was too internally divided to make much of the victory at Lepanto.

The Ottoman fleet was swiftly rebuilt with more modern vessels, though crews proved to be more of a problem due to the massive losses at Lepanto. More significantly, the Ottoman fleet no longer seemed invincible and although it enjoyed successes after 1571, it was no longer supreme.

The Turks lost at Lepanto because their tactics failed to keep pace with the development of weapons technology. As a result they were forced to fight in a way that exposed them to the enemy's powerful guns, which could often prevent a boarding and inflict massive damage on a vessel trying to engage in a firefight.

LEPANTO

KEY

◀ CHRISTIAN FLEET

◀ OTTOMAN FLEET

1 Don Juan's squadrons move into the Gulf of Patras toward the Turk's anchorage, protected by towers and shore artillery. The Christian formation becomes a crescent with the horns toward the enemy.

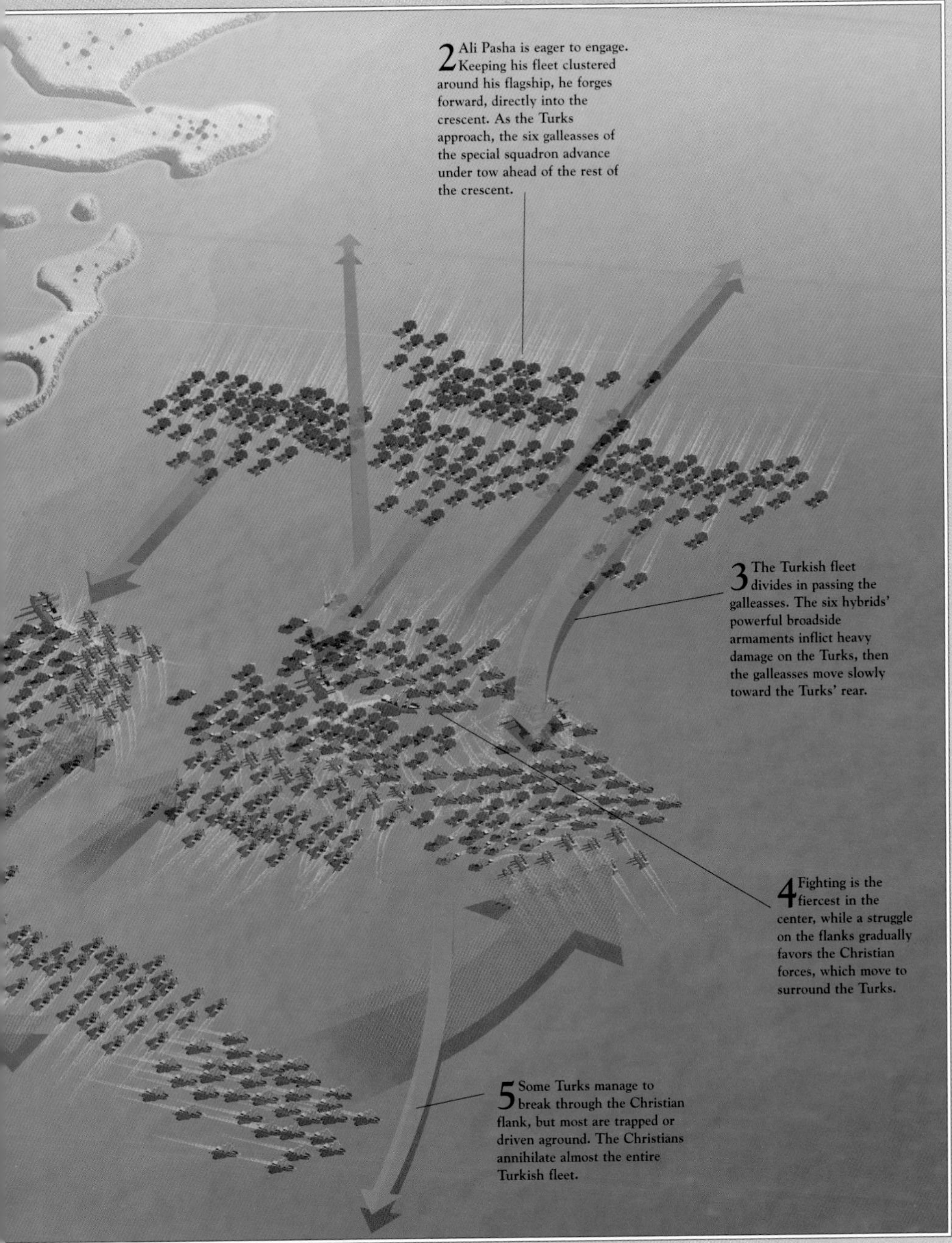

2 Ali Pasha is eager to engage. Keeping his fleet clustered around his flagship, he forges forward, directly into the crescent. As the Turks approach, the six galleasses of the special squadron advance under tow ahead of the rest of the crescent.

3 The Turkish fleet divides in passing the galleasses. The six hybrids' powerful broadside armaments inflict heavy damage on the Turks, then the galleasses move slowly toward the Turks' rear.

4 Fighting is the fiercest in the center, while a struggle on the flanks gradually favors the Christian forces, which move to surround the Turks.

5 Some Turks manage to break through the Christian flank, but most are trapped or driven aground. The Christians annihilate almost the entire Turkish fleet.

SPANISH ARMADA

1588

King Philip II of Spain (1527–98), confident that he was executing the will of Almighty God, went to war against England in 1585. A devout Roman Catholic, Philip's intent was clear. Protestant England and its heretic Queen Elizabeth I (1533–1603) must be returned to the papal fold while Spanish sovereignty in Flanders must be affirmed.

Philip, King Consort of England until the death of his wife, Queen Mary I (1516–58), might even claim the English throne. Mary, the Catholic half-sister of Elizabeth, had ordered the execution of approximately 300 non-Catholics during her reign and is known to history as Bloody Mary.

To achieve his ambitious goals, Philip devised a master plan involving strong forces on land and sea. A mighty fleet, the "Invincible Armada," would sail from the Iberian

SPANISH ARMADA FACTS

Who: The Spanish Armada, 22 galleons and 108 armed merchant vessels commanded by Don Alonso Pérez de Guzmán el Bueno, Duke of Medina Sidonia versus the English Fleet (35 warships and 163 armed merchant vessels) under Charles Howard, Lord High Admiral and Earl of Nottingham.

What: The Spanish attempted to defeat the English fleet and launch an invasion of England.

Where: The waters of the English Channel and the North Sea off the coasts of England and Flanders.

When: July–August 1588.

Why: Spain's King Philip II sought to restore Roman Catholicism in England, halt English raiding of his treasure galleons, and possibly claim the English throne.

Outcome: The Spanish Armada was thoroughly defeated by the English navy in a series of engagements culminating with the battle off Gravelines and then mauled in severe weather during its return odyssey to Spain.

LEFT: A TWISTED LINE OF SPANISH GALLEONS AND ENGLISH FIGHTING SHIPS engage at Gravelines. The Great Armada was then forced to sail around the British Isles to reach Spain.

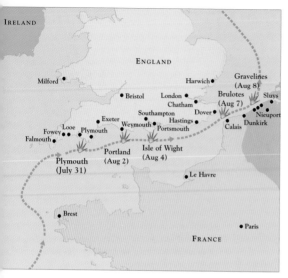

ABOVE: LORD ADMIRAL HOWARD *kept his fleet between the Armada and the vulnerable English coast. English ships and a superior rate of fire were not enough to shatter the Armada's formation or prevent its progress up the Channel—until the fireships and chaos at Gravelines.*

Peninsula into the English Channel, defeat any naval force sent against it, and eventually land troops on English soil. The Armada would further screen a large army, which was to cross the Channel from Flanders and invade England. Meanwhile, Elizabeth offered support to a Protestant uprising in Flanders; defied the will of Pope Sixtus V (1521–90), who excommunicated her; and authorized the beheading of her cousin, the Catholic Mary Queen of Scots (1542–87), in retribution for promoting subversive activities.

PAINFUL PREPARATIONS

Philip's grand design was agonizingly slow in taking shape. The 150 ships of the formidable fleet, commanded by Alvaro de Bazan, the Marquis of Santa Cruz (1526–88), had to assemble from several locations and included sailors of numerous nationalities. Communications with Philip's ground commander in Flanders, Alexander Farnese, Duke of Parma (1545–92), would be difficult at best.

To complicate matters, veteran English seaman Sir Francis Drake (1540–95) raided the Spanish anchorage at Cadiz in the spring of 1587, sinking more than 20 ships. The Marquis was tardy in his pursuit of Drake, and when he finally set sail the fleet was buffeted by strong storms. When his battered ships returned to port, the exhausted Marquis fell ill and died in February 1588. His replacement was a reluctant Don Alonso Pérez de Guzmán el Bueno, Duke of Medina Sidonia (1550–1615). Despite an obvious

SPANISH SOLDIER

Warrior in the wetlands, this light infantryman in the Duke of Parma's invasion force faced the swamps, the elements, and the Dutch in the course of Spain's long and, in the end, doomed struggle to maintain supremacy over the Netherlands. A brass morion helmet, traditionally associated with Spain, protects his head. A padded jerkin offers less protection and lighter weight than the traditional back-and-breastplate of the heavier troops. Next to his canteen dangle wooden cartridges with powder and ball to pour into the bore of his caliver, a lighter, musket-sized version of the more famous and much heavier arquebus. A long sword stands ready as his final recourse should the battle come to close quarters in a lack of ammunition or a chance to reload.

lack of experience, Medina Sidonia led 130 ships, approximately 60 of them vessels intended for combat, to sea from the port of Lisbon on May 28. Aboard were a complement of 8,000 sailors and 19,000 infantrymen. While Parma was aware that the Armada was en route and had 30,000 soldiers standing ready in Flanders, he was uncertain as to when Medina Sidonia would arrive.

THE ENGLISH WAIT

In harbor at Plymouth, the English fleet, which ultimately numbered as many as 200 ships although a relative few were combat vessels, waited for the Invincible Armada to appear on the horizon. In overall command of the British naval force was Charles Howard, Lord High Admiral and Earl of Nottingham (1536–1624), who was capably supported by squadron commanders Drake, Martin Frobisher (1535–94), and John Hawkins (1532–95).

Hampered by bad weather, the Spanish Armada did not arrive off the English coast until the middle of June. On the 19th, the enemy ships were sighted off Cornwall, and a warning was flashed to the defending fleet and the court of Elizabeth I in London via a system of beacons. More than 50 English warships weighed anchor to confront the invaders.

DOCTRINE OF DEFEAT

Although their vast fleet made an imposing sight, the Spanish would soon discover that their tactics and equipment were outmoded and inferior. Their galleons were large, unwieldy vessels, difficult to sail, particularly in the narrow waters of the English Channel with its shoals and shifting currents. They were constructed with "castles" fore and aft to house large contingents of fighting men, and their cannon were a hodgepodge of varied types that fired unreliable shot.

The Spanish gun crews were hardly even taught how to reload. Such a skill seemed unnecessary because the idea was to come to close quarters with the enemy, fire a single broadside, grapple, and board. After firing a cannon shot, the gunners became boarders who were to fight hand-to-hand. In contrast,

ABOVE: QUEEN ELIZABETH I OF ENGLAND INSPIRED HER SUBJECTS to resist the overwhelming might of the Spanish enemy and authorized naval commanders to harass Spanish shipping.

Elizabethan England maintained no standing army. Its warships were crewed by dedicated sailors, who efficiently serviced their cannon. The English fighting ships were smaller, of shallower draft, and much faster than the ponderous Spanish galleons. Taking advantage of their more nimble vessels, the English captains intended to stay on the weather gauge of the enemy fleet, keeping a safe distance and pounding the Spanish with accurate cannon fire.

RUNNING ENGAGEMENTS

For several days, the English probed the fighting capabilities of the Armada during indecisive clashes. On July 31, the Spanish maneuvered into battle formation, two wings, each of 20 or more ships, supporting a main force of about 36 galleons arrayed to protect the transports. In battle lines, Drake and Howard were unable to inflict major damage. Near Eddystone and Portland, the adversaries fought inconclusive actions. Off the Isle of Wight on August 4, the English prevented Medina Sidonia from safely anchoring and forced him back to the open sea in order to avoid running aground. Nevertheless, two galleons did just that.

Eventually, the Spanish anchored in a great crescent off the Flemish coast near Dunkirk, where Parma's army was camped. There was no available harbor large enough to shelter them, and Howard ordered eight fireships, which had been packed with tar, pitch, and gunpowder, loosed against them. Two of these were taken in tow and led away, but one Spanish ship caught fire and several were compelled to cut their cables and sail out of harm's way.

Finally, after sparring for nearly three weeks, the opposing fleets came to blows once again on August 8. Off Gravelines in Spanish-occupied Flanders, the agile English employed

BELOW: A GUN DECK FROM THE MARY ROSE, which sunk decades before the Armada encounter, is typical of the larger warships of the era. Heavy guns low in the hull provided stability, but the high castles above the spar deck were enough to heel the galleon over sufficiently for water to flow into her gunports and sink her. Her successors would lack the top clutter but emulate her layered gun decks.

ABOVE: JOHN HAWKINS WAS KNIGHTED for his role in defeating the Spanish Armada. He also assisted in designing new English warships.

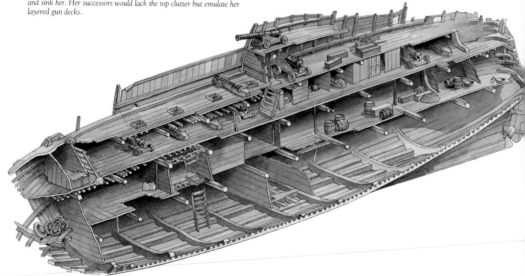

disciplined fire, allowed the Spanish to loose their single broadside, and then closed to more favorable range. Estimates of Spanish ships lost in the fight are as high as 11, with at least two run aground and more than 800 men dead. The following day, their ammunition nearly depleted, the English pursued their enemy into the North Sea and away from any hope of assisting Parma in an invasion.

THE ARMADA'S ANTICLIMAX

Faced with the prospect of running the English gauntlet or sailing a circuitous route around Scotland and Ireland to reach safety, Medina Sidonia chose the latter. Encountering vicious storms, the Armada was chewed like a bone, and many of its galleons were dashed against the rocks of the Irish coast. Thousands more men died when their ships sank.

Months after undertaking its foray against England, the remnants of the Armada, only 67 battered and beaten ships, reached the safety of Spanish waters. More than 8,000 of its sailors were dead, wounded or suffering from illness. English casualties had amounted only to about 500 as a result of the fighting, but many more were to suffer and die from disease.

Although England had been saved from invasion and the House of Tudor would remain on the throne of Protestant England, the war with Spain dragged on for 18 more years. By the time the conflict ended, both Philip II and Elizabeth I were dead. The defeat of the Spanish Armada, perhaps accomplished as much by harsh weather conditions as English seamanship, remains one of the most famous engagements in military history. For some, it ranks as equal with the Battle of Britain nearly 350 years later as England's finest hour.

BELOW: THE VAST SIZE AND EQUIPMENT of the Spanish Armada made England's doom seem certain, but standardized calibers on wheeled gun carriages kept the Spanish out to sea and Elizabeth on the throne.

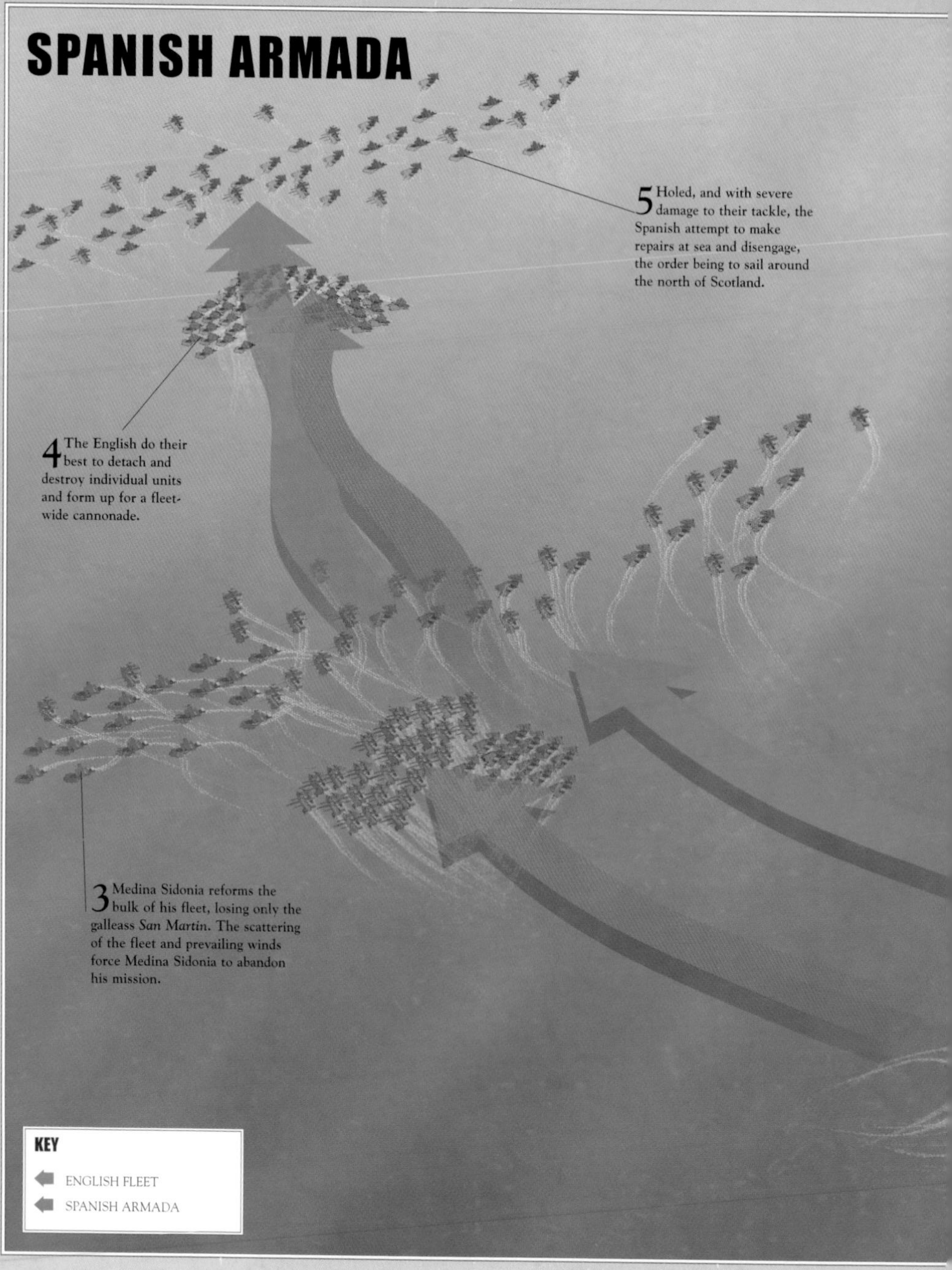

SPANISH ARMADA

5 Holed, and with severe damage to their tackle, the Spanish attempt to make repairs at sea and disengage, the order being to sail around the north of Scotland.

4 The English do their best to detach and destroy individual units and form up for a fleet-wide cannonade.

3 Medina Sidonia reforms the bulk of his fleet, losing only the galleass *San Martin*. The scattering of the fleet and prevailing winds force Medina Sidonia to abandon his mission.

KEY

⬅ ENGLISH FLEET

⬅ SPANISH ARMADA

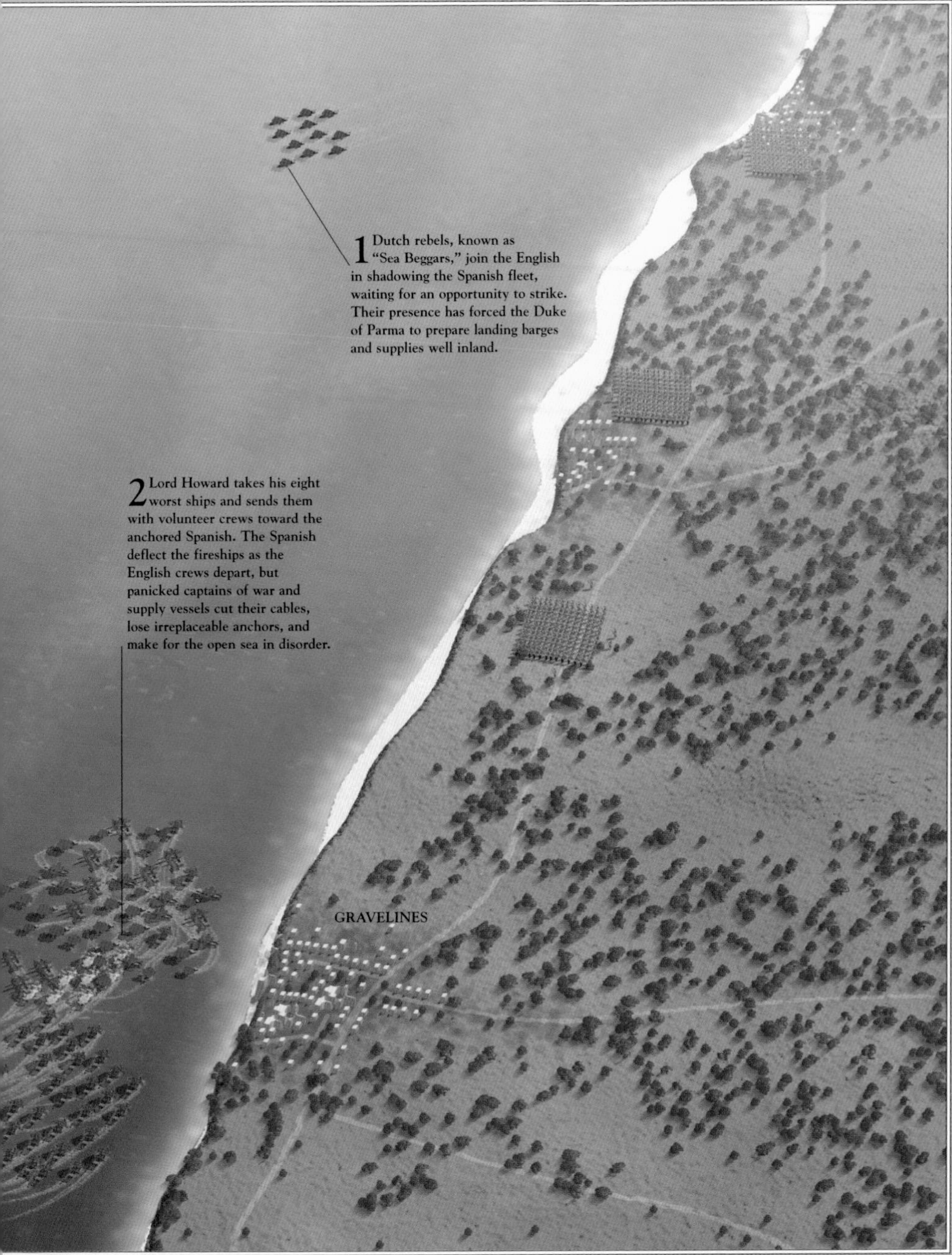

1 Dutch rebels, known as
"Sea Beggars," join the English
in shadowing the Spanish fleet,
waiting for an opportunity to strike.
Their presence has forced the Duke
of Parma to prepare landing barges
and supplies well inland.

2 Lord Howard takes his eight
worst ships and sends them
with volunteer crews toward the
anchored Spanish. The Spanish
deflect the fireships as the
English crews depart, but
panicked captains of war and
supply vessels cut their cables,
lose irreplaceable anchors, and
make for the open sea in disorder.

GRAVELINES

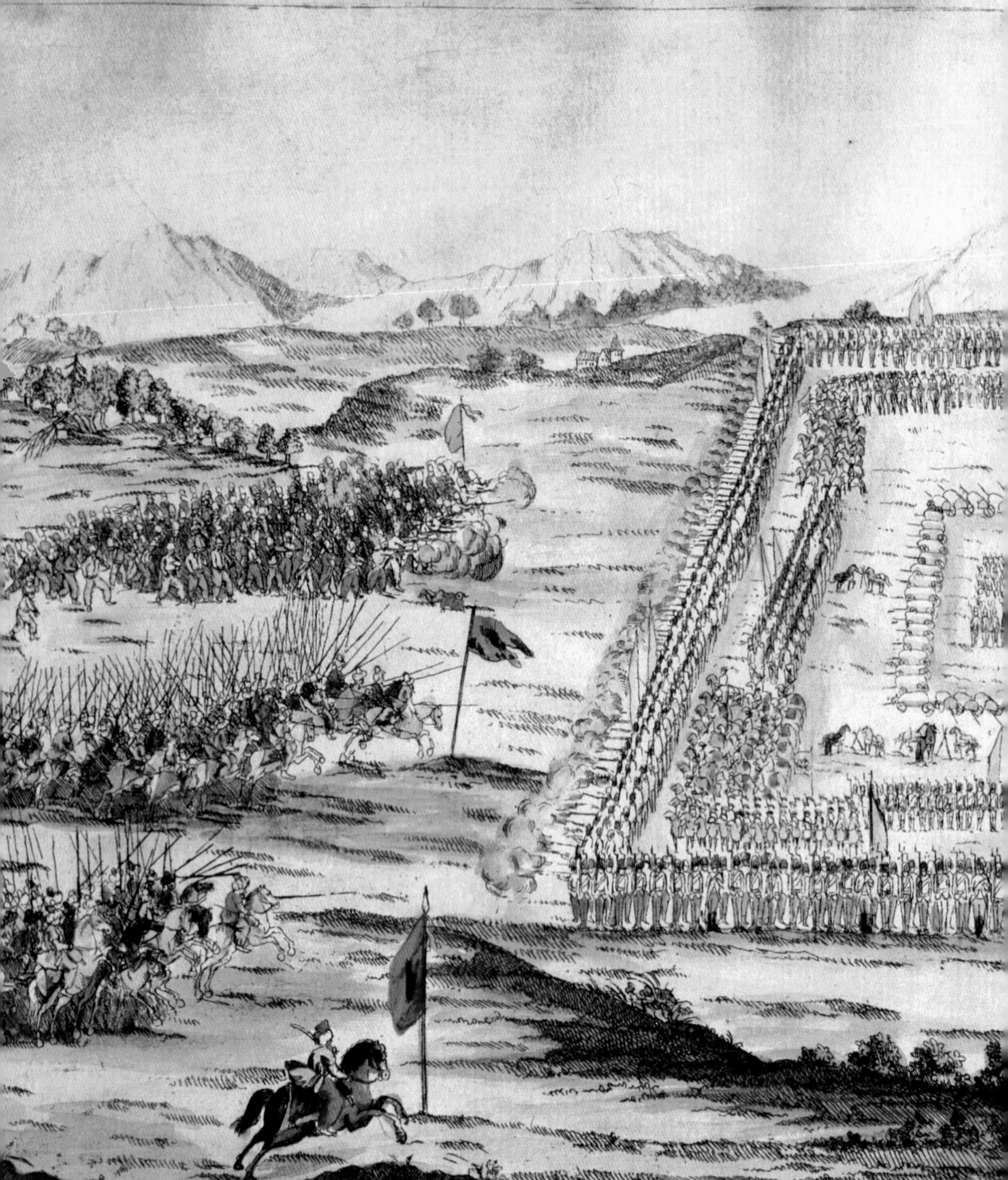

ff der Türken auf die Avantgarde der G. F. M.
sie am 15ten Oct. von Novi nach Neugradisha in

KARÁNSEBES 1788

For a battle to take place, there normally have to be two or more opposing forces present. This was not the case at the "Battle" of Karánsebes, which was simply an escalating self-inflicted disaster of incredible proportions.

onflict between Turkey and Austria was nothing new when war broke out in 1787. At that time, Austria was allied to Russia. The Ottoman Emperor, who sought war with Russia in order to regain territories previously ceded by treaty, did not know this, however. This in turn triggered the Austro-Russian alliance and brought Turkey and Austria into conflict.

The war did not go well for Turkey or Austria. Turkish military operations were bungled or failed for lack of supplies and planning, while Austrian troops died by the thousands in epidemics that swept through the army. Despite some Turkish successes early on, the war ended with the loss of more territory to Russia. Austria gained little, and morale at home was shattered not only by

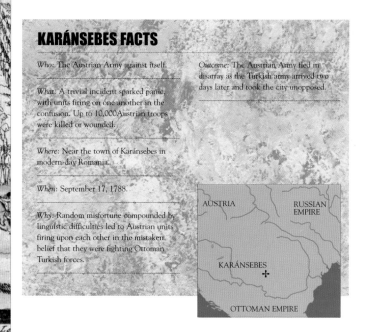

KARÁNSEBES FACTS

Who: The Austrian Army against itself.

What: A trivial incident sparked panic, with units firing on one another in the confusion. Up to 10,000 Austrian troops were killed or wounded.

Where: Near the town of Karánsebes in modern-day Romania.

When: September 17, 1788.

Why: Random misfortune compounded by linguistic difficulties led to Austrian units firing upon each other in the mistaken belief that they were fighting Ottoman Turkish forces.

Outcome: The Austrian Army fled in disarray as the Turkish army arrived two days later and took the city unopposed.

> AUSTRIA
>
> RUSSIAN EMPIRE
>
> KARÁNSEBES ✝
>
> OTTOMAN EMPIRE

LEFT: TURKISH CAVALRY CHARGE AN AUSTRIAN CAMP *defended by infantry drawn up in square. The Austrians had good cause to fear the Turkish cavalry.*

HUNGARIAN HUSSAR

The Austrian Empire recruited troops from all corners of its wide territory. Among them were Hungarian Hussars (meaning horsemen, but originally it is thought to have meant bandits) who served as light cavalry and army scouts. Notorious for their indiscipline, Hussars had a propensity to loot and plunder wherever they went.

Originally the Hussars fought in small bands of irregulars. Over time they were reorganized into larger, more organized formations with a uniform based on their flamboyant traditional dress, and armed with a curved saber augmented by pistols and carbines.

ABOVE: AN AUSTRIAN CORPORAL TYPICAL OF THE INFANTRY of the period. He is armed with a musket and bayonet, backed up by a short hanger (a small sword) for close-quarter fighting.

disease but also by the disaster at Karánsebes on September 17, 1788.

THE AUSTRIAN ARMY IN 1788

The Austrian Empire recruited its troops from all over its territory, as large empires are wont to do. As with other such forces, this created problems with communication between ranks. The officers were mainly Austrian but their troops might be drawn from an entirely different background. In many units officers and men communicated through a small number of interpreters, whose grasp of at least one of the tongues in use might be vague.

There were also political problems arising for the same reason. The Austrian officer class had little in common with their men, and the language barrier served only to make the division harder to cross. Senior officers were seen as aloof and uninterested in the welfare of their troops, which was probably a fair judgment. Political problems also existed between units of different nationalities. Although they served alongside one another, many of the ethnic groups within the Austrian army disliked or even hated one another. Old enmities surfaced from time to time in the form of bitter disputes, and even when the troops were not actively at one another's throats there was little inclination to support and rely on one another.

Senior leadership did nothing to improve this situation. With strenuous effort it might have been possible to build ties of loyalty between officers and men, and between different ethnic groups serving the same cause. There was no such effort, however. Even if they were aware that such problems existed, senior officers were more concerned with their status in society than dealing with the problems of a hopelessly fragmented army.

THE WAR OF 1787–91

When fighting broke out between Russia and Turkey in 1787, Austria dutifully declared war on Turkey in support of her ally and assembled an army for campaign. Joseph II (1741– 90), the Holy Roman Emperor, led it, but even though he greatly admired the brilliant Prussian king Frederick the Great (1712–86), Joseph was entirely incapable of emulating his prowess on the battlefield.

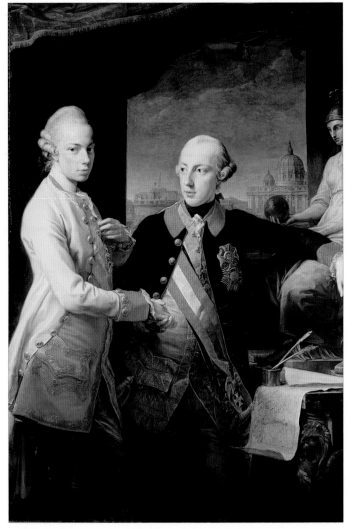

ABOVE: EMPEROR JOSEPH II AND GRAND DUKE LEOPOLD OF TUSCANY. *The Emperor was a very poor commander placed in charge of a disorganized army. The results were predictable.*

The Austrian army advanced with the intention of intercepting a Turkish advance on the fortress of Vidin, located on the southern bank of the Danube River in northwestern Bulgaria. As usual, scouts were pushed out ahead of the army to search for the enemy. For this purpose, the Austrian army used hussars.

Hussars were irregular light cavalry whose flamboyant manner and colorful dress inspired many other nations to raise light cavalry formations and name them after the Austrian hussars. Properly handled, they could be very

effective as scouts and to harass an enemy. In battle they were best suited to screening, flanking, and pursuit of a beaten foe. Unfortunately, hussars could also be unruly and difficult to control. Indeed, many scholars believe that the origin of the word hussar comes from a Balkan word for a mounted bandit. As the Austrian army reached the Timis River, a party of hussars was sent across the bridge at

ABOVE: AN AUSTRIAN DRAGOON. *Dragoons evolved over time from mounted infantry into an arm of the heavy cavalry, though in some nations they were still expected to be able to fight on foot.*

Karánsebes to search for the enemy. They did not find any evidence of the Ottoman army, which was still two days' march away, but they did encounter a group of Wallachian gypsies who offered to sell them schnapps. Naturally the hussars accepted the offer and quickly became drunk.

CHAOS AT KARÁNSEBES

As the hussars were making merry with their new gypsy friends, a group of infantry arrived and, understandably, wanted to join the party. Cavalry and infantry have often failed to get along even in cohesive forces, and the Austrian army was anything but that. The hussars refused and chased off the newcomers. Determined to get their share of the booze, some of the infantry pressed the issue but were

repelled by drunken and aggressive cavalrymen. Some of the hussars fired their weapons at the attackers, who replied in kind. Other infantrymen came up with a clever ruse to scare off the cavalry by pretending that either they were Turks or that the Turks were approaching.

This did not work quite as planned. Instead of frightening the hussars, the ruse alarmed other infantry nearby who had heard the shots. It was dark, and a fight seemed to be going on nearby so these men became nervous.

An Austrian officer tried to restore sanity, shouting "Halt!" in German, but this sounded somewhat like "Allah!" to some of those who heard, further reinforcing the idea that the advanced forces were under attack. Frightened men began firing at dimly seen figures in the dark, some of them entirely imaginary, while others fled back toward the camp of the main army.

THE BATTLE INTENSIFIES

Some of those who fled were mounted, and according to certain accounts the firing caused several carthorses to break loose and stampede through the camp. Men were shouting in several languages, often unable to tell what anyone else was saying. Hearing horses racing through the camp, a senior officer ordered his artillery to open fire and repel what he thought was a major cavalry attack. The cannon had no clear target but fired at any movement that seemed threatening, and by this time infantrymen were doing the same. With the camp in chaos and on fire in places, men did what they felt necessary to save themselves.

Individuals and small groups fled or tried to make a stand, firing at anyone who approached them. In the darkness it was impossible to tell that what seemed to be a charging enemy was actually a terrified friend, nor that other groups trying to protect themselves from imaginary attack fired the bullets that tore across the camp. Taking casualties from what appeared to be enemy musketry, those groups that had stood their ground returned fire in the general direction the shots had come from.

Some men ran wild as discipline broke down entirely. Soldiers raped and looted in the nearby villages, burning houses in an orgy of pointless destruction. The Austrian army dissolved into a chaotic maelstrom of fleeing men and others fighting with all the savagery of cornered rats to defend themselves. The Emperor himself was pushed from his horse and fell into a stream. It was not until the next morning that the true picture began to emerge. The army had simply turned on itself in panic and inflicted a spectacular defeat.

OUTCOMES

The Austrian army arrived at Karánsebes 100,000 strong. It lost one-tenth of its manpower during one night, taking into account dead, wounded, and missing soldiers, some of whom simply melted away into the countryside. The camp was largely destroyed and supplies were lost.

The Ottoman army reached Karánsebes two days later. By that time the Austrian army, its morale shattered and its units still in total disarray, had retreated. The town was taken without opposition. The incident that started the "battle" could have happened in any army, but the nature of the Austrian Empire at the time, and its military forces in particular, contributed greatly to the level of catastrophe that followed. Lack of trust between officers and men, and between units of different nationalities, made it unlikely that discipline would hold, and linguistic problems made it impossible to restore order.

ABOVE: THIS AUSTRIAN GRENADIER is armed with an eighteenth century musket. The long sword at his side suggests he is a noncommissioned officer.

BELOW: AUSTRIAN CAVALRY OVERRUN A TURKISH CAMP in 1790. Some of the Turkish infantry have had time to form defensive squares. The rest are ridden down or sabered.

KARÁNSEBES

MORAVIA

AUSTRIA

CROATIA

BUDAPEST

5 Marshal Laudon, returning from retirement, leads an Austrian campaign to recapture Belgrade. The tide begins to turn against the Ottoman Empire and its army threatens to mutiny.

BANAT

BELGRADE

SERBIA

3 The Turks take advantage of the situation, capturing the Banat region in 1789 and making other gains against fragmented and inept opposition. Disease sweeps through the Austrian army.

KEY

◄ OTTOMAN TURKS

◄ AUSTRIAN/RUSSIAN FORCES

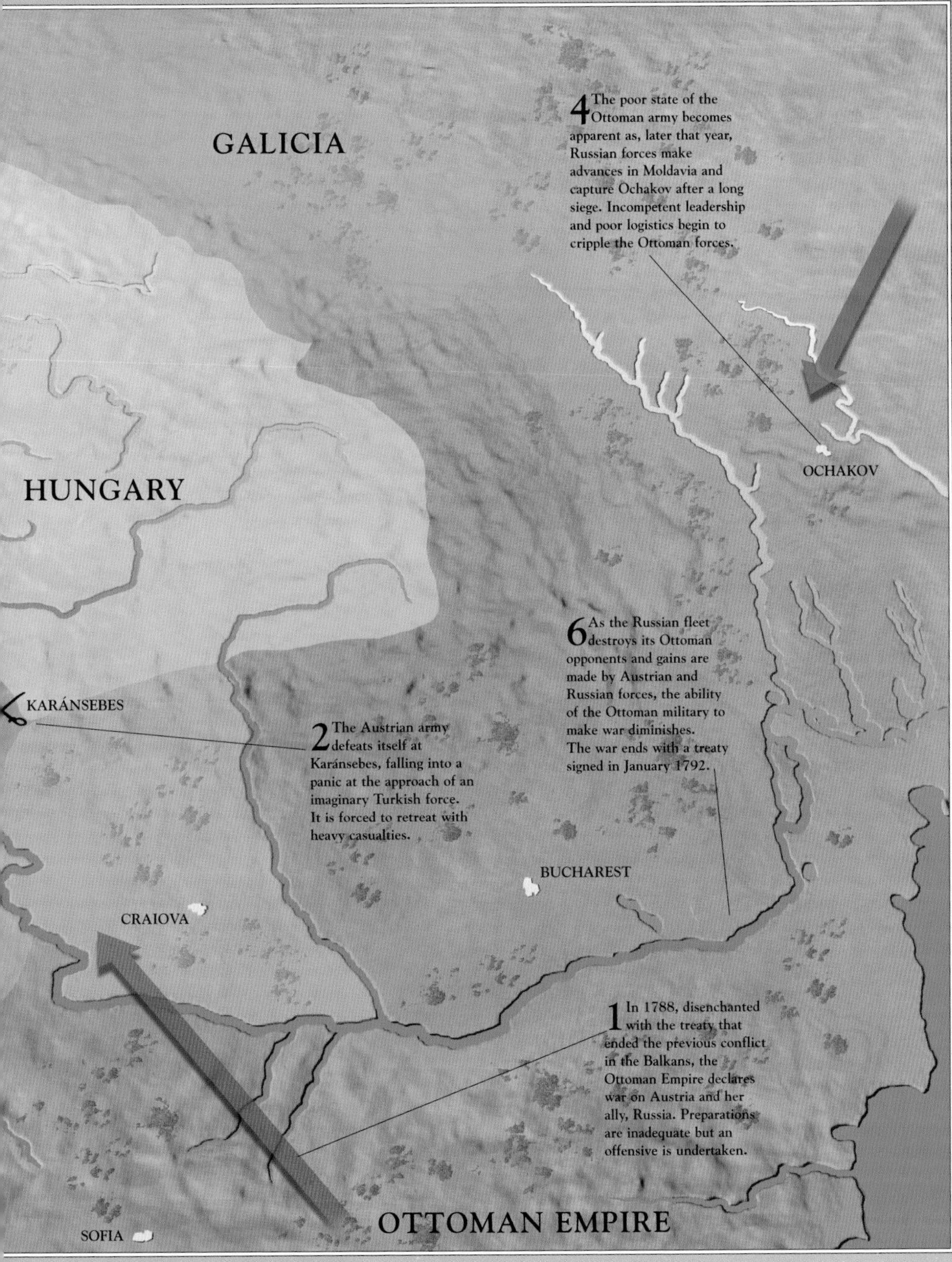

GALICIA

4 The poor state of the Ottoman army becomes apparent as, later that year, Russian forces make advances in Moldavia and capture Ochakov after a long siege. Incompetent leadership and poor logistics begin to cripple the Ottoman forces.

HUNGARY

OCHAKOV

6 As the Russian fleet destroys its Ottoman opponents and gains are made by Austrian and Russian forces, the ability of the Ottoman military to make war diminishes. The war ends with a treaty signed in January 1792.

KARÁNSEBES

2 The Austrian army defeats itself at Karánsebes, falling into a panic at the approach of an imaginary Turkish force. It is forced to retreat with heavy casualties.

BUCHAREST

CRAIOVA

1 In 1788, disenchanted with the treaty that ended the previous conflict in the Balkans, the Ottoman Empire declares war on Austria and her ally, Russia. Preparations are inadequate but an offensive is undertaken.

SOFIA

OTTOMAN EMPIRE

RETREAT FROM MOSCOW
1812

Emperor Napoleon is sometimes known as the "Great Gambler." Many of the risks he took paid off handsomely, but the invasion of Russia in 1812 was an unmitigated disaster. The French Grande Armée was destroyed by cold, hunger, and attrition rather than a decisive battle.

After the Battle of Friedland in 1807, Russia and France entered into an alliance, which many Russians considered to be one-sided. By 1810 the Czar Alexander I (1777–1825) had begun to ignore some of the terms of the Treaty of Tilsit, which defined the alliance. In 1812 Napoleon (1769–1821) decided that the arrangement no longer suited his purposes and launched a massive invasion of Russia.

Napoleon's strategy for dealing with international crises was straightforward. He would march into the target country and try to bring about a decisive battle in order to destroy the country's military capability. This might be enough to force a treaty favorable

MOSCOW FACTS

Who: The French *Grande Armée*, numbering around 600,000 men, under Emperor Napoleon opposed by three Russian armies and a large number of partisan and irregular forces, totaling 900,000 men in all.

What: Having captured Moscow, the French were forced to retreat in the depths of winter.

Where: The main French line of advance was via Vilna (modern-day Vilnius, Lithuania) and Smolensk toward Moscow. The retreat followed a similar route.

When: June to December, 1812.

Why: Napoleon hoped to force a treaty on the Russians by taking Moscow.

Outcome: The *Grande Armée* was ruined and the seeds of Napoleon's final defeat sown. Military losses amounted to 300,000 French and 260,000 allied troops. Russian losses are thought to be similar.

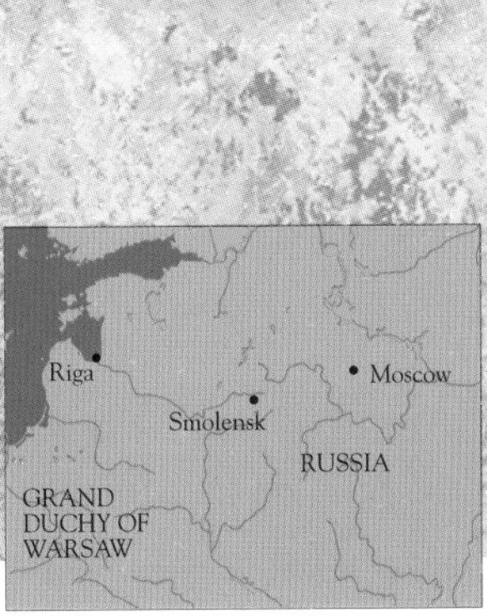

LEFT: NAPOLEON'S RETREAT FROM MOSCOW as painted by Warsaw-born artist Jan Chelminski (1851–1925). The retreat was hard for the Imperial Guard, but the rest of the Grande Armée suffered worse.

ABOVE: REJECTING A FLANKING MANEUVER, Napoleon attacked head-on at Borodino but failed to gain the decisive victory the French needed.

BELOW: PROTECTED BY AN ARMORED CUIRASS (breastplate) and helmet, and armed with a straight thrusting sword, the French cuirassier was a potent force on the battlefield.

to France on the defeated nation. If not, Napoleon would advance on the enemy capital and dictate terms from there.

This approach was risky but it had worked in the past, allowing him to become the master of Europe. However, Napoleon was aware of the military power of Russia and the considerable distance he would have to advance through hostile territory. His nearest bases were in Poland, and it was there that the *Grande Armée*—more than 600,000 men—was assembled.

Extensive preparations were obviously necessary, and Napoleon gave the appropriate orders. Observers marveled at the way these instructions were rattled off in a logical and workable sequence, with considerable attention to detail and great precision. However, it was one thing to give guidelines for quantities of shoes and ammunition to be prepared and positioned; obtaining these items proved more of a challenge.

Nevertheless, with his supply train rather less comprehensive in reality than on paper, Napoleon gave the order to move eastward. He did not at that time intend to advance on Moscow but expected a decisive battle early in the campaign.

THE ADVANCE

Although Imperial Russia could muster large numbers of troops, these were not concentrated and the individual forces could not halt the French. Attempts to concentrate and establish a good position were defeated by the speed of the French advance, forcing the Russians to fall back.

The French did not have it all their own way, of course. Harassment by Cossacks and regular cavalry was a serious nuisance, and the forage was very poor. This was a major problem because the French army had developed a tradition of living off the land as it marched, and this was not possible in Russia. Bad roads made the advance a constant struggle, but nevertheless momentum was maintained.

By the time the French reached Vilna (modern-day Vilnius, capital of Lithuania) the supply situation was becoming dire, largely because of a "scorched earth" policy implemented by the retreating Russians. Men had to be detached to guard the line of supply while the logistics troops did their best to bring up food and supplies from the magazines far away in Poland. The *Grand Armée* was losing men at an alarming rate despite not fighting a major battle.

The Russians attempted a stand at Smolensk and then fell back again. At the village of Borodino, some 75 miles (120 km) from Moscow, they assembled sufficient troops in a good enough position and offered battle.

THE BATTLE OF BORODINO

Early in his career Napoleon had been a master of maneuver, but by 1812 he had acquired a habit of using his army as a battering ram. The capture, on September 4, 1812, of the Shevardino Redoubt (a fortified position built in front of the main defensive line) necessitated a hurried Russian redeployment. Consequently their left flank was weak.

However, despite suggestions of a flanking attack by his subordinates, Napoleon settled on the unimaginative plan of a frontal assault, and on September 7, 1812, the Battle of Borodino, bloodiest clash of the Napoleonic Wars, began.

The Russians held a good position, with their front protected by ravines and woods. A Great Redoubt (a temporary but solidly constructed defensive position) and smaller field fortifications (called flèches) had been constructed, and it was against this formidable position that the French hurled themselves.

The main Russian line at the flèches was broken after bloody fighting, with the fortifications changing hands several times. Consolidating this position, the French then had to break a second line anchored on the Great Redoubt. By the time this position was taken, the day was almost over, and the Russian army withdrew.

Although possession of the battlefield is a traditional measure of victory, there was little to choose from between the two sides. Both had lost 30,000–40,000 men, which the Russians were better able to replace. However, the Russian army retreated and Napoleon was able to lead his army on to Moscow without much further opposition.

DISAPPOINTMENT IN MOSCOW

Napoleon expected the Czar to surrender when he took Moscow, but instead he found that most of the population had fled, taking with them anything edible. Not only was the capture of the city an anticlimax, it created new problems. Winter was closing in and French troops were forced to forage for whatever they could find in the city. Fires broke out, whether deliberately or otherwise, and without strong civil authorities in place to handle the crisis, they soon got out of control. As much as 80 percent of the city was destroyed.

Bereft of victory, food, and shelter, Napoleon made the decision to retreat. He had intended to follow a different route to that he had approached Moscow along, marching

ABOVE: EMPEROR NAPOLEON IN MILITARY UNIFORM. *By 1812 he was past his best and willing to buy victory at the cost of heavy casualties.*

FRENCH SOLDIER

The "French" soldier might in fact have been recruited from almost any part of Napoleon's vast European empire. Former enemies of France fought alongside French troops with considerable gusto, even enduring the appalling conditions of the Moscow campaign.

This soldier's thick greatcoat also serves as a blanket. A cover to reduce damage on campaign protects his hat. Other equipment is minimal, enabling the French army to march quickly, so long as it is possible to forage for supplies along the way. Although an asset in most campaigns, reliance on living off the land led to disaster in Russia.

through lands not stripped of forage by his army and the Russian scorched-earth policy. However, the vanguard was unable to break through Russian forces, which were forming blocking position, and the army was channeled back along its former route.

RETREAT FROM RUSSIA

Forced to retreat through a barren area, the French army gradually disintegrated as cold, hunger, and attacks by irregular forces took their toll. Men who had deserted or straggled from the army during its advance now contested the few sources of food available.

Formations shrank or broke up entirely, though some retained their cohesion right to the end. Similarly, some commanders rallied what men they could find and formed a scratch rear guard that helped protect the others.

There were few major actions, though a Russian attack as the army tried to cross the Berezina River caused major casualties. In truth there was no need to fight another battle; the French were losing massive numbers of men every day. About 30,000–40,000 troops reached French territory in

BELOW: IT HAS BEEN CLAIMED the Russians torched Moscow to deny it to the French, or that the French burned Moscow to punish the Czar.

ome semblance of military order, and roughly the same number came out of Russia as stragglers. The *Grande Armée* had essentially ceased to exist.

OUTCOMES

The 1812 invasion of Russia shattered the Napoleonic myth of invincibility, and cost the French Empire a significant proportion of its military manpower. Worse was the political cost. Previously docile territories began to rebel and a French general attempted a coup in Paris. Napoleonic France was able to somewhat recover from this blow, but it was the beginning of the end. After Moscow the odds were simply stacked too high against the Great Gambler.

Napoleon fell victim to "mission creep" in his invasion—he had not intended to go all the way to Moscow and was not prepared for the task. Supply arrangements that were barely adequate for the invasion as planned were simply not up to the challenge imposed upon them.

Had the Czar surrendered at Moscow as expected, things might have been different, but perhaps not. The French army had taken a lunge at victory and, when its enemy moved out of range, it had no choice but to keep going forward until it was impossibly overstretched across the vast expanse of land that made up western Russia. Losses would have been significant even had the army been able to find billets and food in a surrendered Moscow.

ABOVE: THE FRENCH ARMY LOST most of its cavalry and draft horses in Russia. Some froze or starved to death, others were eaten by troops.

ABOVE: A RUSSIAN COSSACK CAVALRYMAN armed with saber and lance. Cossacks harassed the Grand Armée during the advance and retreat, for the most part picking off stragglers and small parties.

RETREAT FROM MOSCOW

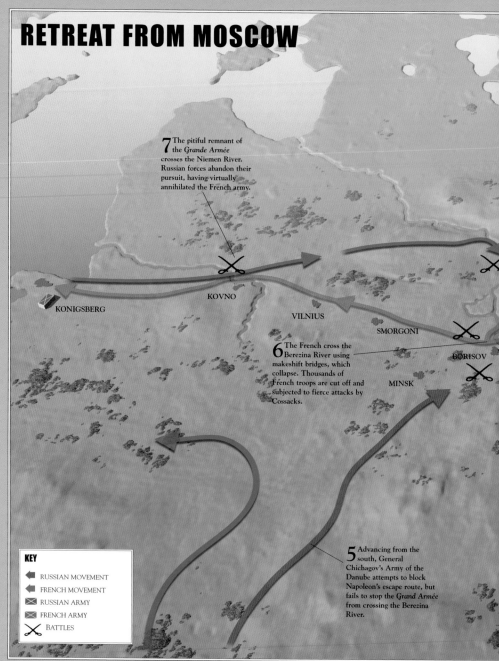

7 The pitiful remnant of the *Grande Armée* crosses the Niemen River. Russian forces abandon their pursuit, having virtually annihilated the French army.

KONIGSBERG

KOVNO

VILNIUS

SMORGONI

BORISOV

MINSK

6 The French cross the Berezina River using makeshift bridges, which collapse. Thousands of French troops are cut off and subjected to fierce attacks by Cossacks.

5 Advancing from the south, General Chichagov's Army of the Danube attempts to block Napoleon's escape route, but fails to stop the *Grand Armée* from crossing the Berezina River.

KEY

- ◄ RUSSIAN MOVEMENT
- ◄ FRENCH MOVEMENT
- ✕ RUSSIAN ARMY
- ✕ FRENCH ARMY
- ✕ BATTLES

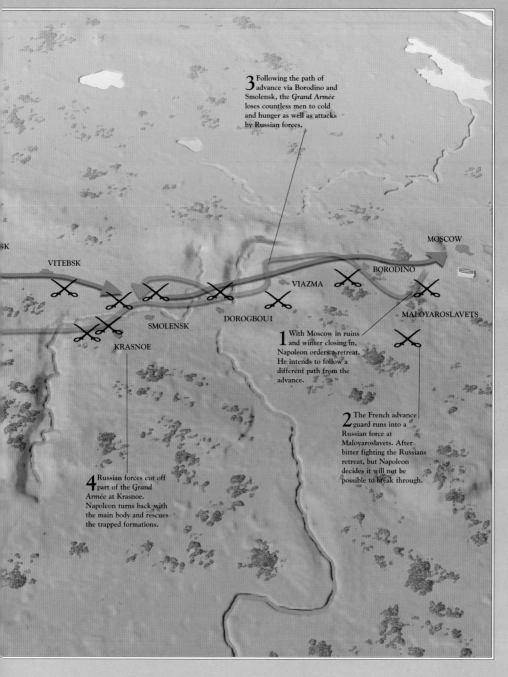

3 Following the path of advance via Borodino and Smolensk, the *Grand Armée* loses countless men to cold and hunger as well as attacks by Russian forces.

MOSCOW

VITEBSK

BORODINO

VIAZMA

SMOLENSK

DOROGBOUI

MALOYAROSLAVETS

KRASNOE

1 With Moscow in ruins and winter closing in, Napoleon orders a retreat. He intends to follow a different path from the advance.

2 The French advance guard runs into a Russian force at Maloyaroslavets. After bitter fighting the Russians retreat, but Napoleon decides it will not be possible to break through.

4 Russian forces cut off part of the *Grand Armée* at Krasnoe. Napoleon turns back with the main body and rescues the trapped formations.

SAN JACINTO 1836

Considering the size of the opposing forces, the Battle of San Jacinto might, at first glance, appear to have been no more than a skirmish. Only about 2,300 soldiers, both Mexican and Texan, were involved, and its duration of less than 20 minutes was remarkably brief. When it was over, however, perhaps no other battle in history had involved so few and produced such far-reaching consequences.

General Antonio López de Santa Anna (1794–1876), the self-proclaimed "Napoleon of the West," controlled the government of Mexico in the years following its independence from Spain. During the same period, settlers from the territory of the neighboring United States relocated in large numbers to the northern Mexican province of Coahuila y Tejas. The government of Santa Anna steadily became more autocratic, suspending the country's constitution, levying high taxes, and eventually prohibiting further settlement by non-Mexicans in Texas.

SAN JACINTO FACTS

Who: The army of Texas with 900 men commanded by Sam Houston versus the Mexican army with 700 men under Antonio Lopez de Santa Anna.

What: Houston seized the initiative, and his charging soldiers virtually wiped out the Mexican force.

Where: Harris County, Texas, near the site of modern-day Houston.

When: April 21, 1836.

Why: Santa Anna hoped for a decisive victory over the rebellious Texans.

Outcome: Santa Anna agreed to withdraw Mexican troops from Texas, which remained independent until annexed by the United States.

LEFT: MEXICAN SOLDIERS PANIC *and flee for their lives before the onslaught of the Texans at San Jacinto in this painting by Henry A. McArdle completed in 1898. The Texans exacted revenge for massacres at the Alamo and Goliad.*

of ultimate victory, advanced toward a showdown with Houston, he was required to maintain lengthy lines of supply and communication. Directly in the path of his army, at San Antonio, stood a tiny Roman Catholic mission called the Alamo. A small contingent of only 183 defenders, commanded by Colonel William Barret Travis (1809–36), occupied the mission. Among them was a band of volunteers from Tennessee led by the famed adventurer and former U.S. Congressman Davy Crockett (1786–1836). Santa Anna was obliged to reduce the Alamo, concerned that bypassing the garrison and leaving a hostile force of any size in his rear presented too great a risk.

For 13 days, the Alamo withstood attacks by overwhelming numbers of Mexican soldiers. Eventually, the walls of the mission were breached, and the defenders were slaughtered to a man. Santa Anna considered his opponents to be traitors, and a number of prisoners were executed on the spot.

Later that month, a Texas army under Colonel James Fannin (1804–36) surrendered at Coleto Creek, the culmination of a series of defeats inflicted by Mexican troops under Santa Anna's subordinate General José de Urrea (1797–1849). Expecting to be treated as prisoners of war, the Texans were marched to Goliad unaware that Santa Anna had issued orders for the execution of all those captured. Urrea's plea for leniency fell upon deaf ears. On Palm Sunday, March 27, 1836, Fannin and 341 others were herded together and brutally massacred.

PANIC AND PATIENCE

News of the atrocities at the Alamo and Goliad spread like wildfire, enraging some Texans who knew they were fighting for their very lives. Other settlers were panic stricken. A frantic evacuation known as the "Runaway Scrape" ensued, and a

ABOVE: MEXICAN SOLDIER. *The uniform of the soldier of Santa Anna's Mexican army may have been more suited to the parade ground than the battlefield.*

Amid the perceived oppression of Santa Anna, a national identity began to stir among the Texans, and open rebellion broke out in the fall of 1835. In March of the following year, delegates gathered at Washington-on-the-Brazos, drafted a declaration of independence, and elected David G. Burnet (1788–1870) President of the Republic of Texas. While the convention was underway, Santa Anna and his powerful army had already moved northward.

MEMORABLE MASSACRES

Few in number and relatively untrained, the main Texan army, commanded by Sam Houston (1793–1863), needed one thing more than any other—time. As long as Houston's army lived, so did the fledgling independent Texas. As Santa Anna, confident

ABOVE: THE ALAMO, *a Spanish mission, became a thorn in Santa Anna's side and the site of a massacre that enraged independence-minded Texans.*

ABOVE: *Davy Crockett's Last Stand at the Alamo with a handful of Texans has become a part of American mythology.*

number of Houston's soldiers deserted to tend to their families during the flight from the marauding Mexicans.

Despite the major setbacks already suffered, Houston was continually urged to fight. Instead, the commander chose the tactic of protracted retreat, drawing the Mexicans deeper into Texas. Santa Anna's army, Houston reasoned, would tire on the long march, while the length of the Mexican supply lines would impede their progress. At the height of the Runaway Scrape, Burnet ordered the evacuation of the Texas capital at Washington-on-the Brazos, relocating the government to Galveston.

Houston knew that troops of the U.S. Army had been positioned along the border with Louisiana to prevent a Mexican incursion into U.S. territory; therefore, he headed for the Sabine River. He was compelled, however, to turn southeast toward the coast as Santa Anna crossed the Brazos River in pursuit of Burnet.

DIVIDED AND CONQUERED

Realizing that the opportunity existed to capture both the rebel government and destroy the Texan army in the field, Santa Anna divided his force into three columns with the third

assigned the task of guarding his supply trains. In doing so, Santa Anna apparently failed to grasp that the destruction of Houston's army would have rendered Burnet's government irrelevant anyway.

In the middle of April, Houston reached a plantation belonging to a wealthy sympathizer named Jared Groce (1782–1839), where he received food and provisions, including lead for the making of musket balls. In addition, a pair of small cannon dubbed the Twin Sisters arrived. These guns, a gift from the citizens of Cincinnati, Ohio, exemplified the support the Texans received from the United States. Indeed, hundreds of volunteers, including militia units from Georgia and Kentucky, had ventured west to fight for the independence of Texas. As the hour of the decisive Battle of San Jacinto approached, Houston counted just over 900 soldiers in his army's ranks.

DAY OF RECKONING

After weeks on the march, Santa Anna and 700 footsore soldiers finally made contact with Houston on April 19 at Lynch's Ferry near the banks of the San Jacinto River and ringed by marshy wetlands. There, he was reinforced by more than 500 troops commanded by General Martín Perfecto de Cos (1800–54), and the Mexican numbers neared 1,400. When he learned of the arrival of Cos, Houston ordered Vince's Bridge, eight miles

(13km) to his rear and the only avenue of approach or retreat for either army by land, destroyed. Meanwhile, Santa Anna believed Houston was trapped and could be annihilated at leisure. Rather than attacking immediately, he ordered his position fortified with a barricade of crates and baggage.

Faced with yet another command decision, Houston held a council of war on the morning of April 21. Against the advice of his officers, he opted to assume the offensive. At 3:30 P.M., the Texas infantry stepped off, quietly closing on the Mexican

TEJANO VOLUNTEER

A company of *Tejano* soldiers— Texans of Mexican descent— was raised by patriot Juan Seguin. This unit fought for an independent Texas in several battles, including the Alamo and San Jacinto. The *Tejano* volunteers also served as scouts for the army of Sam Houston during the revolution. This *Tejano* is carrying a single-shot musket and a knife for defense during close combat.

ABOVE: *THE DEFEATED SANTA ANNA stands before an injured Sam Houston on April 22, 1836, the day after a small force of Texans defeated the Mexican Army at San Jacinto.*

line while about 60 cavalrymen skirted the enemy's left flank. Inexplicably, Santa Anna had failed to post sentries or skirmishers, and as the Texans approached, many Mexican soldiers napped during the afternoon siesta.

SHATTERED SILENCE

Within yards of the Mexican line, the Texans charged, shouting, "Remember the Alamo!" and "Remember Goliad!" Santa Anna's startled soldiers were thrown into confusion. With no time to form ranks, many of them fled in terror without firing a shot. Others fought hand-to-hand with the Texans and were routed. Vigorously pursued, many of them were shot dead or slashed by cavalry sabers as they wallowed in the marshes. General Don Juan Almonte (1803–69) attempted to organize a defense but soon realized the futility of further resistance and surrendered with 400 men. Santa Anna managed

to slip away from the debacle on horseback, wearing the coat of a common soldier. Spurring his men forward, Houston was wounded in the foot by a Mexican bullet.

The frenzied Texans exacted revenge for those murdered at the Alamo and Goliad. In 18 minutes, it was over. The Mexican army had suffered 630 dead, 208 wounded, and 730 captured, while only nine Texans were killed and 30 wounded.

AFTERMATH

The day after his catastrophic defeat at San Jacinto, Santa Anna was captured and brought before Sam Houston, who spared his life in exchange for a pledge that Santa Anna's army would leave Texas. Victory at San Jacinto ensured, at least for a time, the survival of the Republic of Texas, which was later annexed by the U.S. government. In time, vast western lands once belonging to Mexico would constitute all or part of 10 of the United States.

LEFT: SAM HOUSTON SERVED AS GOVERNOR *of both the states of Texas and Tennessee during a long political and military career.*

SAN JACINTO

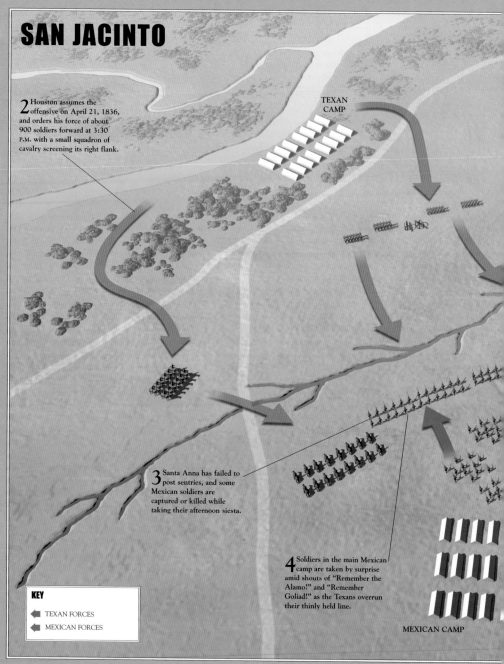

2 Houston assumes the offensive on April 21, 1836, and orders his force of about 900 soldiers forward at 3:30 P.M. with a small squadron of cavalry screening its right flank.

TEXAN CAMP

3 Santa Anna has failed to post sentries, and some Mexican soldiers are captured or killed while taking their afternoon siesta.

4 Soldiers in the main Mexican camp are taken by surprise amid shouts of "Remember the Alamo!" and "Remember Goliad!" as the Texans overrun their thinly held line.

MEXICAN CAMP

KEY

TEXAN FORCES

MEXICAN FORCES

1 Sam Houston learns that the Mexican force near the San Jacinto River is nearly 1,400 strong and orders the destruction of Vince's Bridge to prevent the approach.

5 Panic-stricken Mexican soldiers flee toward the marshes near the edge of the river. Many are shot or sabered as they run. In 18 minutes, 630 Mexicans are killed.

6 Santa Anna narrowly escapes but is captured the following day. In exchange for his life, the Mexican commander pledges to withdraw his army from Texas.

CHARGE OF THE LIGHT BRIGADE 1854

With the outbreak of the Crimean War, the combined forces of Great Britain, France, and Turkey laid siege to the port of Sevastopol at the tip of the Crimean peninsula. The siege was to last a grueling 11 months, and the Russian army mounted two unsuccessful efforts to raise it. The first of these, the Battle of Balaclava, occurred on October 25, 1854.

While powerful Russian forces defended Sevastopol, a large army had evaded encirclement as the British-French-Turkish coalition invested the city in the spring. Prince Aleksandr Sergeyevich Menshikov (1787–1869), commanding the Russian troops at Sevastopol, devised a plan to cut the besieging coalition army off from its supply base at Balaclava some distance away and attack coalition forces facing Sevastopol from the rear.

CHARGE OF THE LIGHT BRIGADE FACTS

Who: The Light Brigade of British cavalry, numbering approximately 670, under the Earl of Cardigan versus an unknown number of Russian cavalry and artillery commanded by General Pavel Liprandi.

What: The Light Brigade charged a mile (1.6km) through enfilading artillery fire to assault Russian positions.

Where: Near the port city of Balaclava in the Crimea.

When: October 25, 1854.

Why: A misunderstood order contributed to the charge, which was initially directed at another objective.

Outcome: The Light Brigade sustained about 40 percent casualties, and the popular poem "Charge of the Light Brigade" by Alfred, Lord Tennyson immortalized the event.

IMPERIAL RUSSIA

Sevastopol • BALACLAVA

• Constantinople

TURKEY

LEFT: AT THE HEIGHT OF THEIR EPIC CHARGE *at Balaclava, cavalrymen of the Light Brigade lash out with sabers at Russian hussars and artillerymen.*

The terrain at Balaclava proved to be a contributing factor in the outcome of the battle. British forces, under the command of Fitzroy Somerset, First Lord Raglan (1788–1855), were positioned in two parallel valleys, each dominated by ridges along their flanks. To the left rose the Fedioukine Hills, while in the center stood the ridgeline called Causeway Heights and to the right were a number of broken hills, ridges, and ravines. The difficulty of tactical control lay in the fact that commanders were often limited in their ability to see the battlefield. Only from the surrounding heights could the unfolding battle be comprehensively viewed.

THE THIN RED LINE

On the morning of October 25, Menshikov's second-in-command, General Pavel Liprandi (1796–1864), ordered 25,000 Russian troops forward against Turkish positions in the southern valley and along Causeway Heights. Attacking at dawn, the Russian infantry made substantial headway, rooting more than 30,000 Turkish soldiers from their trenches and capturing a number of artillery pieces. Soon, Russian cavalry advanced to exploit the breakthrough.

The Russian cavalry split into two columns, the first heading straight for Balaclava. In its path stood the 93rd Highland Regiment. Commanding the kilt-clad Highlanders, Colin Campbell, the First Baron Clyde (1792–1863), formed his troops into two rows. The Scottish soldiers poured telling volleys into the enemy horsemen as they topped a low ridge, standing their ground along what came to be known as "The Thin Red Line."

ABOVE: HOLDING THE "THIN RED LINE," men of the 93rd Highland Regiment pour a devastating fire into charging Russian cavalry at Balaclava.

Within minutes, one of the British cavalry units, the Heavy Brigade, had charged headlong into the second Russian mounted column. The horsemen of the Scots Greys and the Royal Dragoon Guards, 700 strong, slashed through their enemy in an unconventional uphill charge. Under the weight of the onslaught, the Russians were compelled to fall back to the protection of strong artillery positions along the nearby Causeway Heights.

CAVALRY CONFUSION

Surveying the scene from the high ground above the battlefield, Lord Raglan observed that the Russians were attempting to haul away a number of Turkish guns they had seized during the morning action. Therefore, he issued a controversial order, which precipitated the epic charge of the British cavalry's Light Brigade. Subordinate to Lord Raglan was the cavalry commander, George Charles Bingham, Third Earl of Lucan (1800–88), who received the order from the overall commander:

"Lord Raglan wishes the cavalry to advance rapidly to the front, follow the enemy, and try to prevent the enemy carrying

ABOVE: MOUNTED ON HIS CHARGER and preparing to ride into combat with his unit, a dragoon accepts his sword from an attendant.

LIGHT BRIGADE LANCER

A soldier of the 17th Lancers charges forward as a pennon attached to his lance flies in the breeze. The pennon was originally intended to frighten opposing cavalry horses but later became a parade item. At Balaclava, Captain Lewis E. Nolan (1818–54), a promising young officer who was killed in the action, accompanied the 17th Lancers during a part of their epic charge.

away the guns. Horse artillery may accompany. French cavalry is on your left. Immediate."

So read the handwritten note from Raglan to Lucan, who was located with the cavalry in the valley and unable to see the entire battlefield. Written by General Sir Richard Airey (1803–81), the army's Quartermaster General, the order immediately seemed ambiguous to Lucan.

LOST IN TRANSLATION

Captain Lewis E. Nolan (1818–54), a promising young officer, had delivered the order, and when Lucan requested clarification as to which guns were referred to, a heated exchange may have taken place. Nolan was seen making a sweeping gesture with his arm toward Russian guns occupying high ground at the opposite end of the northern valley about a mile away—not the Turkish guns at the Causeway Heights. Such actions could indicate that Nolan himself was confused as to the direction of the assault. In turn, Lucan forwarded the fateful order to James Brudenell, Seventh

ABOVE: THE BRITISH HEAVY BRIGADE also fought a more successful action at Balaclava, chasing the Russian cavalry out of the southern valley.

Earl of Cardigan (1797–1868), commander of the British cavalry's Light Brigade, which consisted of the 17th Lancers, 8th Hussars, 11th Hussars, 4th Light Dragoons, and 13th Light Dragoons. Lucan and Cardigan, incidentally, held each other in great contempt. Cardigan had married, and subsequently separated from, Lucan's youngest sister. Whether their personal animosity had any bearing on the execution of the order is doubtful but cannot be completely discounted. In the event, Cardigan turned to the business at hand, setting the charge of the Light Brigade in motion.

It was said that Cardigan accepted the order as was expected of a good soldier. However, he pointed out that the Russians not only had gun emplacements at the other end of the valley but also along Causeway Heights and the Fedioukine Hills. In fact, more than 50 cannon, along with Russian infantry, were arrayed on three sides of the Light Brigade's proposed route. The response from Lucan was direct. The order had come from the highest echelon of command, and it must be executed.

THE EPIC CHARGE

Numbering about 670, the Light Brigade moved into the valley, Cardigan riding at its head. Captain Nolan joined the charge, accompanying the 17th Lancers. Moments later, Nolan rode directly across the brigade's front as if to indicate that the charge was headed in the wrong direction. If so, it was too late.

For his trouble, a shell fragment killed Nolan, one of the first to fall. Artillery fire rained down from the high ground. Riderless horses, horribly wounded, shrieked as they stumbled through blinding smoke. The dead and wounded lay everywhere. In spite of the horrific losses, Cardigan and the remnants of the Light Brigade ran the Russian gauntlet, actually reaching the guns at the end of the valley. Apparently, he had been unaware of the carnage occurring behind him and was seething with rage at Nolan, whom he assumed had been trying to take over command of the charge.

Many of the Russian gunners were sabered, but the shattered Light Brigade still faced overwhelming odds. From the rear came news that Russian cavalry threatened to cut off the survivors. Forced to retreat, the Light Brigade was supported by the French Chasseurs d'Afrique, who drove the Russians from the Fedioukine Hills and covered the withdrawal. When the battle was over, at least 118 of the brigade were dead and 127 wounded, a casualty rate of nearly 40 percent. The Battle of Balaclava ended with the opposing forces occupying essentially the same ground they had previously held.

AFTERMATH

News of the disastrous charge did not reach England for nearly a month. For years, the various commanders defended their conduct during the series of events that led to the charge. In

ABOVE: IN THIS ROMANTIC PORTRAYAL of the charge of the Light Brigade, hussars and lancers cut their way through the Russian artillery.

the final analysis, there seems to be enough blame to go around. Lucan withheld the Heavy Brigade from supporting the Light and never ordered the specified horse artillery forward. Cardigan did not fully understand his objective and failed to gain clarification from Lucan, who had been unable to discern from Nolan the exact requirement of the order. The order in itself had been vaguely issued by Raglan and inadequately interpreted in writing by Airey.

The most enduring result of the Battle of Balaclava is the poem *Charge of the Light Brigade* by Alfred, Lord Tennyson (1800–92). "Cannon to the right of them/ Cannon to the left of them/ Cannon in front of them…" it reads in part. Truly, the Light Brigade had charged into the "jaws of Death" and gained immortality.

LEFT: FITZROY SOMERSET, FIRST LORD RAGLAN, commanded British forces at Balaclava and issued the order that led to the Charge of the Light Brigade.

CHARGE OF THE LIGHT BRIGADE

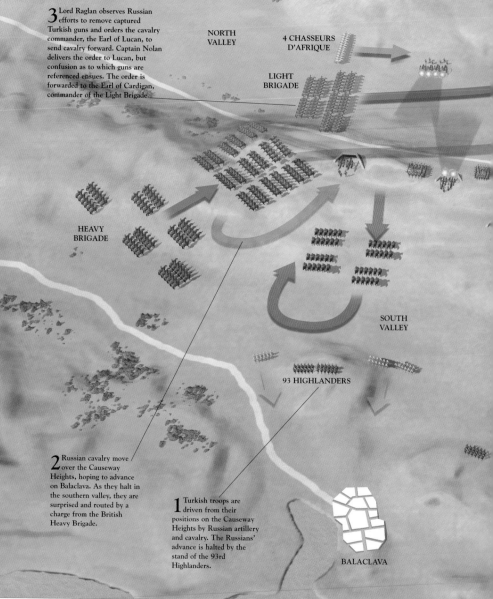

3 Lord Raglan observes Russian efforts to remove captured Turkish guns and orders the cavalry commander, the Earl of Lucan, to send cavalry forward. Captain Nolan delivers the order to Lucan, but confusion as to which guns are referenced ensues. The order is forwarded to the Earl of Cardigan, commander of the Light Brigade.

NORTH
VALLEY

4 CHASSEURS
D'AFRIQUE

LIGHT
BRIGADE

HEAVY
BRIGADE

SOUTH
VALLEY

93 HIGHLANDERS

2 Russian cavalry move over the Causeway Heights, hoping to advance on Balaclava. As they halt in the southern valley, they are surprised and routed by a charge from the British Heavy Brigade.

1 Turkish troops are driven from their positions on the Causeway Heights by Russian artillery and cavalry. The Russians' advance is halted by the stand of the 93rd Highlanders.

BALACLAVA

4 Cardigan is dismayed that 50 Russian guns and a host of infantry occupy three sides of the approach to an artillery position at the far end of the North Valley.

5 Minutes later, the Light Brigade embarks on its epic charge toward Russian artillery positions a mile (1.6km) away. Enemy fire takes a fearful toll. At the height of the charge, British horsemen reach the Russian guns amid terrible carnage, sabering a number of the artillerymen.

CAUSEWAY
HEIGHTS

6 Threatened with being cut off and annihilated, the remnants of the Light Brigade are compelled to retire, having suffered nearly 40 percent casualties.

KEY

RUSSIAN FORCES

BRITISH FORCES

GETTYSBURG 1863

At approximately 3 p.m. on July 3, 1863, nearly 13,000 Confederate soldiers began moving across more than a mile (1.6 km) of open ground, heavily defended by Union artillery and infantry, their objective an isolated copse of trees along the shallow crest of Cemetery Ridge. The three days of the Battle of Gettysburg were, collectively, the bloodiest engagement ever in the Western Hemisphere.

The gallant charge of the divisions of generals George Pickett (1825–75), James Pettigrew (1828–63), and Isaac Trimble (1802–88), has been immortalized as symbolic of the lost cause of the Southern Confederacy. When Pickett's Charge was over, the eventual outcome of the American Civil War would no longer be in doubt.

In the summer of 1863, General Robert E. Lee (1807–70) and the Confederate Army of Northern Virginia embarked on a second invasion of the North in less than a year. The first, in the fall of 1862, had been turned back at the Battle of Antietam in western Maryland. Now, replenished and energized by its stunning

GETTYSBURG FACTS

Who: The Confederate Army of Northern Virginia with a force of 75,000 men commanded by General Robert E. Lee versus the Union Army of the Potomac with a force of 97,000 men under General George G. Meade.

What: The second invasion of the North by the Confederates was turned back, punctuated by the disastrous Pickett's Charge.

Where: The vicinity of Gettysburg in southern Pennsylvania.

When: July 1–3, 1863.

Why: Following a great victory at Chancellorsville, the Confederates hoped to win a major battle on Union soil and threaten northern cities.

Outcome: At the height of its power, the Confederate Army was decisively defeated, and the strategic initiative passed irretrievably to the Union.

GETTYSBURG ✚ • New York
• Washington
• Richmond

LEFT: UNION INFANTRY STAND FIRM *against the Confederates as Pickett's charge is pressed home. The charge was a bloodbath for the Confederates, with Pickett's division suffering 2,655 casualties.*

IRISH BRIGADE

Two soldiers of the Union Army's Irish Brigade prepare to repel a Confederate assault at Gettysburg. The Irish Brigade, which consisted primarily of Irish immigrants, fought bravely in the Wheatfield on the second day of the battle. One of its chaplains, Father William Corby, offered absolution to the troops on the battlefield just before they entered the fighting.

victory at the Battle of Chancellorsville in May, Lee's army advanced into Pennsylvania, carrying the war from beleaguered Virginia to previously untouched Union territory and threatening the cities of Baltimore, Philadelphia, and even Washington, D.C.

As he had done in the past, Lee divided his army, and powerful Confederate forces raided far ahead of his main body. Within three weeks, the bold rebels had occupied York and Carlisle and were in the vicinity of Pennsylvania's capital city, Harrisburg.

RUSH TO JUDGMENT

With his command of nearly 75,000 soldiers spread out over miles of the Pennsylvania countryside, Lee admonished his senior commanders not to bring on a general engagement with Union forces until the Confederate army could be concentrated. Further complicating the situation, Lee's most trusted subordinate, General Thomas J. "Stonewall" Jackson (1824–63), was dead, a victim of friendly fire at Chancellorsville, while his cavalry commander, General J.E.B. Stuart (1833–64), had embarked on a lengthy ride around the Union Army of the Potomac, depriving Lee of information on enemy movements. Meanwhile, just four days prior to the Battle of Gettysburg, a Pennsylvanian, General George G. Meade (1815–72), had been elevated to command of Union forces, 97,000 strong.

The town of Gettysburg had no real strategic value. However, one nearby commodity—shoes—was of great interest to the Confederates, and a detachment was sent to

BELOW: CLAD IN BUTTERNUT AND GRAY, *a skirmish line of lean and ragged but resolute Confederate soldiers stands its ground at Gettysburg.*

ocate them. Instead, the Confederates found Union cavalry, and what began as a skirmish quickly escalated as both sides ed fresh troops into a widening engagement. Neither Lee nor Meade was yet present on the field.

BLOODY BUT INDECISIVE

Throughout July 1, fighting raged across the hills and fields north and east of Gettysburg. By afternoon, the hard-pressed Union troops had been pushed through the streets of the town and assumed defensive positions on high ground at Culp's Hill and Cemetery Hill. As Union forces arrived, their defensive line was extended southward across Cemetery Ridge to the vicinity of Little Round Top. The following day, the battle resumed on the Union left flank at the Peach Orchard, the Wheatfield, and a craggy jumble of boulders known locally as Devil's Den. The Army of the Potomac averted disaster by rushing reinforcements to the summit of Little Round Top moments ahead of advancing Confederate troops. Meade held a war council during the night, and the consensus was to await a renewed attack from Lee.

LONGSTREET'S LAMENT

By July 3, Lee remained resolute. Meade had skillfully defended the high ground and utilized the advantage of

ABOVE: GENERAL GEORGE PICKETT *led his division against the center of the Union line on Cemetery Ridge at Gettysburg, July 3, 1863.*

BELOW: UNION TROOPS KNEEL, AIM, AND FIRE RELENTLESSLY *as Confederate soldiers climb over a stone wall during Pickett's Charge in this detail from the Gettysburg Cyclorama.*

interior lines, and Lee concluded that Meade had sapped the strength of his center.

To take advantage of this perceived weakness, Lee decided to commit his only reserve, Pickett's division, to assault the Union center along Cemetery Ridge. The depleted divisions of Pettigrew and Trimble, elevated when generals Henry Heth (1825–99) and Dorsey Pender (1834–63) were wounded, would provide support. The attack was to take place in concert with a feint by Confederate General Richard Ewell at Culp's Hill and following preparatory bombardment by nearly 150 massed Rebel cannon directed by youthful but brilliant Colonel E. Porter Alexander (1835–1910).

When he was informed of the plan, General James Longstreet (1821–1904), commander of the I Corps, objected strenuously. Longstreet advocated a movement around the Union left flank, which might force Meade to abandon his strong defensive positions. Lee, however, would have none of it. "The enemy is there," he told Longstreet, "and I am going

LEFT: UNION GENERAL GEORGE MEADE'S *headquarters, behind the line on Cemetery Ridge, came under Confederate fire prior to Pickett's Charge.*

BELOW: CONFEDERATE GENERAL LEWIS ARMISTEAD, *his hat perched atop his drawn sword, leads surging soldiers at The Angle during Pickett's Charge.*

o strike him." Convinced that an assault against the Union enter was doomed to fail, Longstreet unenthusiastically rdered preparations. Contrary to Lee's wishes, Ewell's action ad waxed and waned before the attack on Cemetery Ridge as undertaken.

At approximately 1 P.M., the thunder of Confederate annon shattered the eerie silence that had descended across he battlefield. Nearly 80 Union guns replied. As his mmunition supply was depleted, Alexander sent an urgent essage to Pickett. The time had come.

HE ILL-FATED CHARGE

heir flags unfurled, the Confederates stepped out of the voods along Seminary Ridge and advanced toward the opse of trees more than a mile (1.6 km) distant. To the Jnion defenders, the sight was awe-inspiring. As if on arade, Pickett's troops executed orders to close a gap with Pettigrew on the left. Quickly, they came under artillery fire rom Union batteries at Culp's Hill, Little Round Top, and long Cemetery Ridge. Shells tore great gaps in the ranks, nd on the left flank one advancing brigade was taken under fire and routed.

The advance was slowed by a rail fence running the ength of the Emmitsburg Road, and as the distance closed Union artillery was joined by rifle fire from more than 5,000 oldiers packed behind a low stone wall and along the shallow rest of Cemetery Ridge. On Pickett's right, a Vermont rigade flanked the advancing column and poured a murderous re into the Confederates. Two of Pickett's brigade ommanders, generals Richard B. Garnett (1817–63) and

James L. Kemper (1823–95), were shot down. The third, General Lewis A. Armistead (1817–63), waving his hat atop his drawn sword, breached the Union line with about 150 men where the stone wall took a sharp, 90-degree turn known to history as "The Angle." Armistead shouted, "Come on boys! Give them the cold steel! Who will follow me?" and fell dead as he placed his hand on a Union cannon.

No Confederate reinforcements were available to exploit the breakthrough, and those not already killed or wounded began streaming back the way they had come. In the span of 20 minutes, nearly 6,500 men had been lost in the disastrous charge, and the high tide of Confederate arms had begun to recede. Union dead and wounded totaled about 1,500. Witnessing the carnage, a despondent Lee rode out to meet his returning soldiers. "It is all my fault," he said. When Lee ordered Pickett to organize his division against the threat of a Union counterattack, Pickett responded, "General, I have no division."

EPILOGUE

The following day, Lee's army began its forlorn trek southward across the Potomac and into Virginia. From Gettysburg to surrender at Appomattox nearly two years later, the Confederacy was obliged to fight a defensive war. Coupled with a crushing defeat in the West at Vicksburg, the decisive battle at Gettysburg sealed the fate of the Confederacy. Pickett and his gallant men had lost their fight but gained everlasting fame.

BELOW: UNION ZOUAVES DISPLAY THEIR MUSKETS, *complete with fixed bayonets. The Zouaves' dress was based on French uniforms of North African origin, and were popular because of the loose, comfortable pants.*

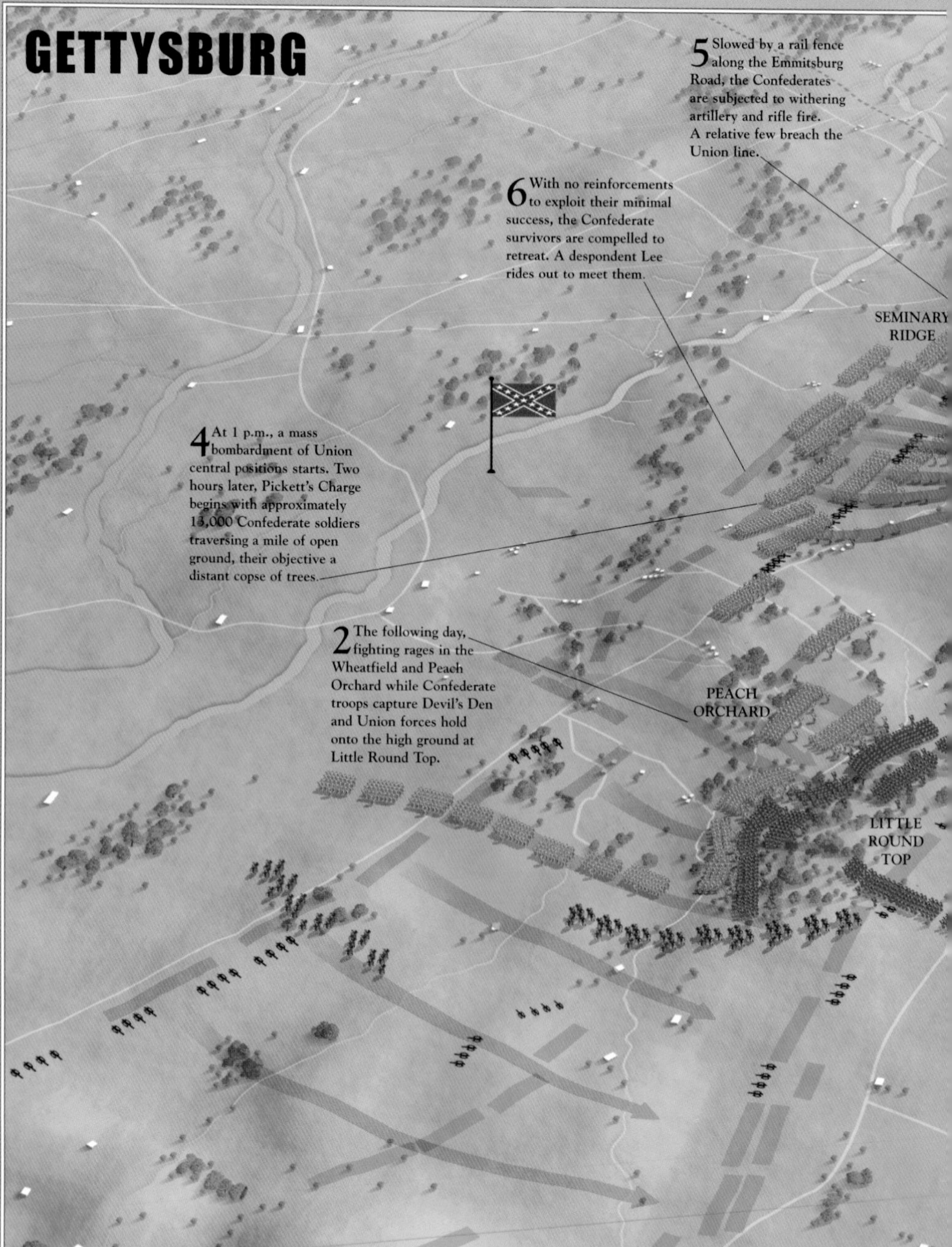

GETTYSBURG

5 Slowed by a rail fence along the Emmitsburg Road, the Confederates are subjected to withering artillery and rifle fire. A relative few breach the Union line.

6 With no reinforcements to exploit their minimal success, the Confederate survivors are compelled to retreat. A despondent Lee rides out to meet them.

SEMINARY RIDGE

4 At 1 p.m., a mass bombardment of Union central positions starts. Two hours later, Pickett's Charge begins with approximately 13,000 Confederate soldiers traversing a mile of open ground, their objective a distant copse of trees.

2 The following day, fighting rages in the Wheatfield and Peach Orchard while Confederate troops capture Devil's Den and Union forces hold onto the high ground at Little Round Top.

PEACH ORCHARD

LITTLE ROUND TOP

1 In the gathering darkness of July 1, Confederate General Richard Ewell fails to seize the heights of Culp's Hill and Cemetery Hill.

GETTYSBURG

CEMETERY HILL

CULP'S HILL

CEMETERY RIDGE

3 General James Longstreet objects to Robert E. Lee's decision to assault the Union center on July 3, but nevertheless sets the plan in motion.

ROCK CREEK

KEY

CONFEDERATE FORCES

UNION FORCES

SEDAN   1870

Within weeks of declaring war on Prussia and her allied German states, Emperor Napoleon III (1808–73) and France were in dire straits. A succession of Prussian victories had thwarted Napoleon's plan to invade Germany and achieve territorial and political concessions through force, which France could not gain through diplomacy.

Wary of the growing might of a unifying Germany, forged primarily by the will of Prussian Chancellor Otto von Bismarck (1815–98), the French had witnessed a dazzling Prussian defeat of Austria in 1866. The disposition of the disputed provinces of Alsace and Lorraine remained contentious, and Prussia had blocked a French attempt to purchase Luxembourg from the Netherlands. Adding to French uneasiness, the Prussians supported the accession of Prince Leopold (1835–1905), a relative of the German House of Hohenzollern, to the throne of Spain. Under French pressure, German Kaiser Wilhelm I (1797–1888) withdrew direct support for Leopold but refused to guarantee that Leopold would not take the

SEDAN FACTS

Who: The 120,000-man French Army of Chalons, commanded by General Patrice de MacMahon versus the 250,000 soldiers of the armies of Prussia and allied German states, commanded by General Helmuth von Moltke.

What: Initially marching to raise the siege of Metz, French forces were encircled and defeated.

Where: The fortress city of Sedan in the valley of the Meuse River.

When: September 1, 1870.

Why: After their defeat at Beaumont, the French retreated, facilitating General Moltke's plan for an encirclement.

Outcome: German victory in the Franco-Prussian War became a foregone conclusion. With the fall of the French Second Empire, the Third Republic was established.

LEFT: *Prussian infantry advance against French North African Zouaves at Sedan on September 1, 1870. The battle ended in disaster for France, and Emperor Napoleon III was captured.*

Spanish throne in the future. It appeared that France was being supplanted as the dominant power on the European continent, and Napoleon III, much to Bismarck's delight, declared war on the Germans on July 19, 1870.

SETBACK AFTER SETBACK

For Napoleon III, his declaration resulted in the debacle of the Franco-Prussian War. Within two weeks, the German army, composed primarily of Prussians, Saxons, and Bavarians, was on the march. The French suffered their first major defeat at Weissenburg in Lower Saxony on August 4, and by the 18th the Germans had won victories at Woerth, Spicheren, Colombey-Nouilly, Vionville, and Gravelotte.

Following its defeat at Gravelotte, the French Army of the Rhine, commanded by Marshal Francois Achille Bazaine (1811–88), retired to the fortress city of Metz, where the Germans surrounded its 150,000 soldiers. In haste, Marshal Patrice MacMahon (1808–93) and the Army of Chalons, 120,000 strong and accompanied by Napoleon himself, advanced to raise the siege.

AN ILL-FATED FORAY

The Army of Chalons marched northeastward toward the Belgian frontier, intending to pivot southward against the Prussians at Metz. The circuitous maneuver, conducted in atrocious weather, served only to degrade the fitness of MacMahon's command while leaving both French flanks exposed to constant harassment. General Helmuth von Moltke (1800–91), chief of staff to Kaiser Wilhelm and principal commander of the German armies, recognized an opportunity to squeeze the French in a giant vise. While the First and Second Prussian armies held Bazaine in check at Metz, the Third Prussian Army and the Army of the Meuse led by Crown Prince Friedrich Wilhelm (1831–88) and Crown Prince Albert of Saxony (1828–1902) respectively, hurried to counter MacMahon.

On August 30, the XII Corps of the Army of the Meuse led by Prince George of Saxony (1832–1904), younger brother of Crown Prince Albert, surprised the French V Corps commanded by General Pierre Louis Charles de Failly (1810–92), at Beaumont. Another French defeat, Beaumont cost the Army of Chalons more than 7,000 killed and wounded along with 42 cannon. Battered and weary, the French fell back near the fortified town of Sedan in the valley of the Meuse River. MacMahon hoped to halt briefly, replenish ammunition, and rest his troops.

Moltke, however, allowed no respite. Maintaining the initiative, the German commander divided his force into three wings, one occupying the French front, a second sweeping to cut off the enemy's line of retreat, and a third maintaining control of the Meuse crossings. When it was

BELOW: DURING FIGHTING AT GRAVELOTTE, wounded French soldiers are tended by medical personnel and nuns from a nearby convent.

ABOVE: *DURING THE FIRST MAJOR BATTLE of the Franco-Prussian War, Prussian forces take the French by surprise at Weissenburg. The Prussian victory facilitated the invasion of France.*

apparent that Moltke had closed a ring of steel around the French army at Sedan, one forlorn French officer remarked, "We are in a chamber pot, and we are about to be covered in excrement."

SWAN SONG AT SEDAN

Slightly after 4 A.M. on September 1, 1870, the decisive battle of the Franco-Prussian War began. Bavarian troops fought the French in the blazing village of Baizelles. Riding forward to assess the situation, MacMahon was wounded by a shell fragment. Command passed to General Auguste-Alexandre Ducrot (1817–82). Two hours later, fighting erupted at La Moncelle on the German right flank, where 72 modern, breech-loading artillery pieces rained destruction on exposed French positions.

Ducrot realized the gravity of the situation, ordering an attempt to break out of the German encirclement and a northward retreat. However, General Emmanuel Félix de Wimpffen (1811–84) arrived and asserted overall command of the French forces. Ducrot's order to withdraw was wholly logical, but the inept Wimpffen immediately countermanded the directive and ordered counterattacks at Baizelles and La

ABOVE: *GENERAL HELMUTH VON MOLTKE, chief of staff to Kaiser Wilhelm, was the principal architect of Prussian victory against the French.*

FRENCH INFANTRYMAN

This French soldier, typical of those who fought during the Franco-Prussian War, prepares to fire his rifle. Uniformed in a slouch hat, greatcoat, and leather boots, he carries a canteen and other accoutrements. At Sedan, inept officers who made poor command decisions in the heat of battle generally led French units. At Sedan, French casualties exceeded 38,000.

Moncelle. Exhibiting more bravado than command sense, Wimpffen snorted, "We need a victory, not a retreat!" The French got neither.

Sometime after 2 P.M., Ducrot, on his own initiative, summoned General Jean Auguste Margueritte (1823–70) and ordered the cavalry commander to ready his *Chasseurs d'Afrique* for a desperate charge against the Prussians at Floing. If the charge was successful, a gap could be opened and what was left of the French infantry might follow to the west.

Margueritte rode ahead to survey the ground and was mortally wounded when a bullet shattered his jaw. The gallant cavalry sallied forth, only to be decimated by concentrated fire from Prussian rifles. Kaiser Wilhelm watched from a distance and could not help but admire the courage of the French. "Ah, the brave fellows," he remarked wistfully. Napoleon III rode through heavy fire during most of the day, ignoring the peril even when one of his entourage was cut in half by a Prussian shell. With his entire army near collapse, the French emperor accepted the counsel of several beseeching generals and authorized them to request surrender terms.

Tightening their grip, the Prussians continued attacking from the east and northwest, while the Bavarians advanced from the southwest. The remnants of the Army of Chalons were herded toward the Bois de la Garenne and Sedan itself. A defiant though incompetent Wimpffen would not accept defeat and led a futile counterattack against the surprised Bavarians at Balan. Temporarily seizing the village, the French could not hold it, and the attack petered out. As Wimpffen withdrew, the white flag of surrender fluttered atop the fortress of Sedan.

IGNOMINIOUS CAPITULATION

The proxies of Napoleon III and Wilhelm I worked out the details of the surrender at Sedan. The French were in no position to negotiate and failed to gain any meaningful concessions from the Germans. Napoleon III became a prisoner of war and was later consoled by Bismarck when the two met after the battle. German casualties were relatively light at Sedan, only 2,320 killed and 5,980 wounded. The French had lost 3,000 dead, 14,000 wounded, and 21,000 captured during the fight. The surrender of the entire Army

BELOW: FOLLOWING THE HUMILIATING DEFEAT at Sedan, French Emperor Napoleon III surrenders to Prussian officers. Defeat in the Franco-Prussian War cost France the provinces of Alsace and Lorraine.

RIGHT: THIS PRUSSIAN INFANTRYMAN wears a garrison cap and carries his distinctive Pickelhaube (spiked helmet) by its leather chinstrap. He has affixed the bayonet to his rifle.

of Chalons placed 83,000 more French soldiers in German captivity. In addition, 449 pieces of field artillery and 139 heavy cannon from the fortifications at Sedan were captured. These may have been of little use to the Germans, since most of the guns were inferior to the Krupp-manufactured weapons they already possessed.

EPILOGUE

When news of the catastrophic defeat at Sedan reached Paris, the Second Empire was doomed. Within months, the Third Republic had been established. The Prussians released Napoleon III, who accepted exile in England. Ironically, the interim government pledged to carry on the war, doing so for another five cruel months.

When the Treaty of Frankfurt ended the Franco-Prussian War on May 10, 1871, France was stripped of Alsace and Lorraine, required to pay financial indemnity, and forced to endure three years of occupation by the Germans. Like the Treaty of Versailles that ended World War I nearly 50 years later, the document which proclaimed peace also sowed the seeds of another conflict.

SEDAN

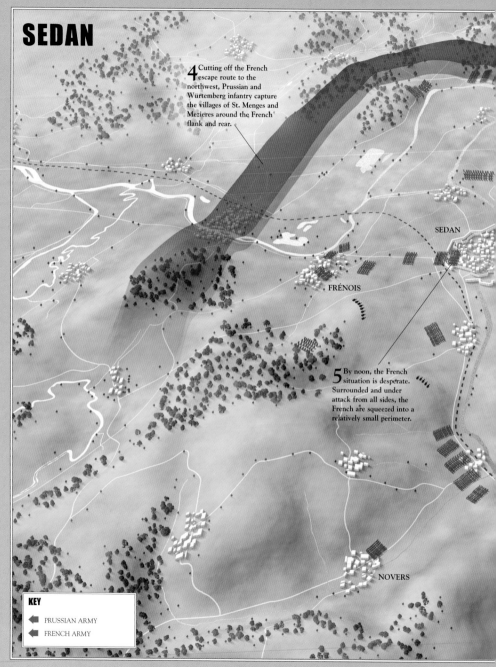

4 Cutting off the French escape route to the northwest, Prussian and Wurtemberg infantry capture the villages of St. Menges and Mezieres around the French flank and rear.

5 By noon, the French situation is desperate. Surrounded and under attack from all sides, the French are squeezed into a relatively small perimeter.

SEDAN

FRÉNOIS

NOVERS

KEY

◄ PRUSSIAN ARMY

◄ FRENCH ARMY

ST. MENGES

3 Modern Prussian artillery, utilizing the new C64 four-pounder gun, decimates a French counterattack launched at 9 A.M. by French North African Zouaves along the Givonne River.

6 The French launch a strong counterattack in an attempt to break out, but Prussian artillery again disrupts the effort. Twelve hours of fighting end with capitulation at 4 P.M.

GIVONNE

VILLERS-CERNAY

BAZEILLES

2 Morning fog lifts, and Bavarian artillery opens in support of infantry attacks by allied German units. Accurate artillery fire hampered French operations throughout the day.

RIVER MEUSE

1 At dawn on September 1, 1870, Prussian infantry launch a strong attack against the elite French *Infanterie de Marine* at the town of Bazeilles.

DOUZY

LITTLE BIG HORN

1876

Few characters in American military history have been as romanticized and as controversial as Lieutenant Colonel George Armstrong Custer (1839–76). During the American Civil War, he earned a reputation as a bold, aggressive commander. Often considered impetuous and vainglorious, Custer apparently did not shun the limelight. Nor did he fail to take advantage of an opportunity to achieve lasting fame.

In 1868, during the Indian Wars, Custer led the 7th Cavalry Regiment in an attack on a Cheyenne encampment at the Battle of the Washita River. He later commanded troops in the Dakota and Montana territories and fought the Sioux at the Battle of the Tongue River in 1873. On June 25, 1876, Custer was in command of the 7th Cavalry in the valley of the Little Big Horn River, in the eastern Montana

LITTLE BIG HORN FACTS

Who: The U.S. 7th Cavalry Regiment commanded by Lieutenant Colonel George Armstrong Custer versus Cheyenne, Sioux, and Arapaho warriors led primarily by Sitting Bull and Crazy Horse.

What: The battle was the most famous action of the Great Sioux War of 1876–77, and was a remarkable victory for the Lakota and Northern Cheyenne.

Where: The valley of the Little Big Horn River, Montana Territory.

When: June 25–26, 1876.

Why: The battle took place during an effort by the U.S. Government and Army to move renegade Indians to a reservation.

Outcome: Custer and elements of his command were slaughtered in fighting that is popularly known as Custer's Last Stand.

MONTANA

✚ LITTLE BIG HORN

WYOMING

TEXAS

LEFT: THIS ROMANTICIZED DEPICTION of Custer's Last Stand shows the controversial commander in the center of his surrounded command, firing his revolver defiantly.

SIOUX WARRIOR

This Sioux warrior, mounted on a blanket of buffalo hide atop a sturdy horse, is typical of the Plains Indians who fought to maintain their tribal lands against the inexorable westward advance of white settlers. Expert horsemen and deadly with the bow and arrow, Sioux and Cheyenne warriors overwhelmed the U.S. 7th Cavalry at Little Big Horn. This warrior carries his bow and a small shield.

Territory. The events of that day, when the cavalrymen encountered a large Indian village, which included as many as 2,500 Cheyenne, Sioux, and Arapaho warriors, remain shrouded in theory and conjecture. One matter of certainty, however, is that Custer achieved the fame he had long sought, leading much of the 7th Cavalry to a rendezvous with destiny.

RED CLOUD AND RESERVATIONS

In November of 1868, the great Sioux chief Red Cloud (1822–1909) concluded a treaty with the United States, agreeing to relocate much of the Sioux nation into a great reservation that encompassed the Black Hills, land sacred to the Sioux. However, some factions of the Sioux, as well as other tribes, refused to abide by the terms of any treaty while white settlers, moving inexorably westward, continued to encroach on Indian land.

Arapaho Indians, who refused to return to reservations in defiance of the U.S. government, joined renegade Sioux under Sitting Bull (1831–90) and Crazy Horse (1842–77). Although the administration of President Ulysses S. Grant (1822–85) was apparently powerless to stem the tide of white settlers, action was taken against the uncooperative Indians.

In the summer of 1876, cavalry and infantry units under General George Crook (1828–90), General Alfred Terry (1827–90), and Colonel John Gibbon (1827–96) ventured into the Montana Territory to bring Sitting Bull and Crazy Horse to heel. In the middle of June, Crook was surprised to find he was facing a large number of Indians and was fought to a standstill. His command roughly handled, Crook had no choice but to regroup.

Meanwhile, Terry and Gibbon combined their forces and continued the offensive. Terry and Gibbon headed directly for the Big Horn and Little Big Horn rivers, while Custer and the 7th Cavalry were ordered to advance along the Rosebud River. If all went according to plan, the Indians would be cornered between the two forces.

CUSTER MOVES FORWARD

On the morning of June 25, Custer received reports that a massive Indian encampment was located roughly 15 miles (24km) away. Although he initially intended to attack on June 26, a subsequent report that approximately 40 Indians had been seen nearby raised concern that the element of surprise had been lost. Custer, therefore, decided to act immediately.

Just after noon, he divided his force into four detachments. The first, led by Custer, counted just more than 200 soldiers. The second included 115 soldiers commanded by Captain

only order of the day to Reno: "Custer says to move at as rapid a gait as you think prudent and to charge afterwards, and you will be supported by the whole outfit."

FATAL FLAWS

Custer has been criticized not only for his bravado and penchant for risk-taking at Little Big Horn, but also for command decisions that had a direct impact on the outcome of the battle. Prior to departing from Terry, Custer was offered the use of the Gatling gun detachment of the 20th Infantry Regiment. He declined, stating that the guns would slow down his advance. He was offered two additional cavalry

BELOW: THIS VETERAN SERGEANT of the 7th Cavalry was typical of the U.S. soldiers who sought to secure the Northern Plains against hostile Native American warriors.

ABOVE: THE FLAMBOYANT GENERAL GEORGE ARMSTRONG CUSTER strikes a pose in full uniform. A veteran of the Civil War, Custer sought lasting fame fighting Native American People.

Frederick Benteen (1834–98), while the third, totaling 142 soldiers and about 35 scouts, was led by Major Marcus Reno (1834–89). The fourth detachment consisted of the regimental train escorted by about 135 soldiers.

Custer and Reno were to ride down the divide between the Rosebud and the Little Big Horn. When the Indian village was sighted, Reno would attack directly. Benteen was to proceed to the left, toward the upper valley of the Little Big Horn, searching for the Indian village and cutting off the most likely escape route. Shortly after 2 p.m., a scout spotted several Indians headed toward the Little Big Horn. When Custer received word, his adjutant delivered his

companies but declined these as well, responding that the 7th Cavalry could handle anything it might encounter. Further, he divided his force of more than 600 cavalrymen into weaker units although he was not certain of the location of the Indian village or the number of warriors he might be facing.

Overconfidence may have contributed to these decisions. Custer had divided his forces and won at the Washita River eight years earlier. In the event, his command faced a hostile Indian force estimated at more than three to four times its number.

CUSTER'S LAST STAND

At about 3 p.m., Reno crossed a small creek, which now bears his name, and attacked the southern end of the Indian village. Quickly, it became apparent that he was confronted by a large contingent of Indian warriors who intended to give battle. Fighting dismounted, the troopers soon gave ground, falling back to a thicket of scrub brush and then to the slopes of a nearby hill. In the confusion, Reno ordered his soldiers to mount, dismount, and then mount again. Although some accused him of faltering under fire, Reno appears to have held his troopers together as well as could be expected.

ABOVE: THIS 1889 LITHOGRAPH OF THE BATTLE OF LITTLE BIG HORN focuses on the final moments of General George Custer and the remnants of his shattered command.

As Reno fell back, Custer committed his two brigades in an assault on the other end of the village. While many of the Cheyenne and Sioux warriors took on this second threat, Crazy Horse led a large force downstream, then doubling back against Custer in a classic envelopment. The hard-pressed cavalrymen were pushed northward to the slope of a long ridge.

Meanwhile, Benteen had advanced 10 miles (16 km) up the valley and found nothing. A scribbled message from Custer hurried him toward the sounds of gunfire. Benteen joined Reno, and following a second day of fighting the remnants of these commands were able to withdraw safely.

Custer, however, had come to grief. His force had been trapped just over three miles (nearly 5 km) from Reno's position and killed to the last man. The actual unfolding of events is sketchy due to the fact that no members of Custer's detachment survived the fighting and the Indians did not record the details. For years, accounts of so-called eyewitnesses were at odds with one another. Modern archeological

investigations reveal that the slaughter, which came to be known as Custer's Last Stand, may have been a running battle rather than that commonly depicted of a prominent Custer and his embattled troopers dying in an ever-tightening ring of Indian warriors.

AFTERMATH

Custer's furious fight for survival may have been short, possibly no more than half an hour in duration. More than 260 soldiers and civilians were dead, and 55 wounded, while casualties among the Indians are estimated at 130 killed and 160 wounded. At length, the cause of the Indians of the Northern Plains was doomed. The army campaign continued, compelling most of them to accept the inevitable and settle on the great reservation. The legend of Custer, or the Son of the Morning Star, as the Indians called him, has been embellished by popular culture and romanticized through the lens of history.

BELOW: A MEMORIAL WAS ERECTED TO MARK the last stand and death of Colonel Keogh and his men at Little Big Horn.

LITTLE BIG HORN

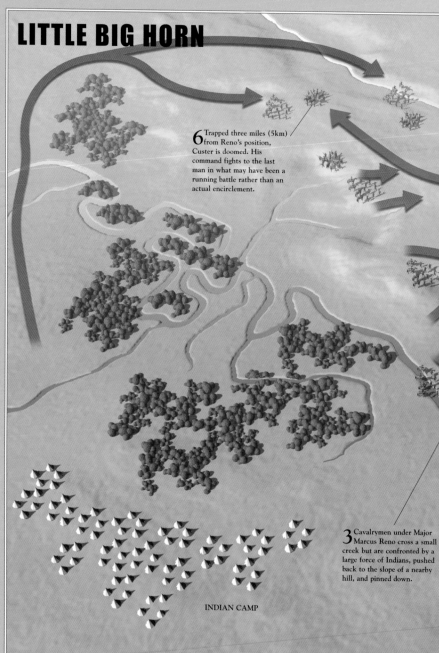

6 Trapped three miles (5km) from Reno's position, Custer is doomed. His command fights to the last man in what may have been a running battle rather than an actual encirclement.

3 Cavalrymen under Major Marcus Reno cross a small creek but are confronted by a large force of Indians, pushed back to the slope of a nearby hill, and pinned down.

INDIAN CAMP

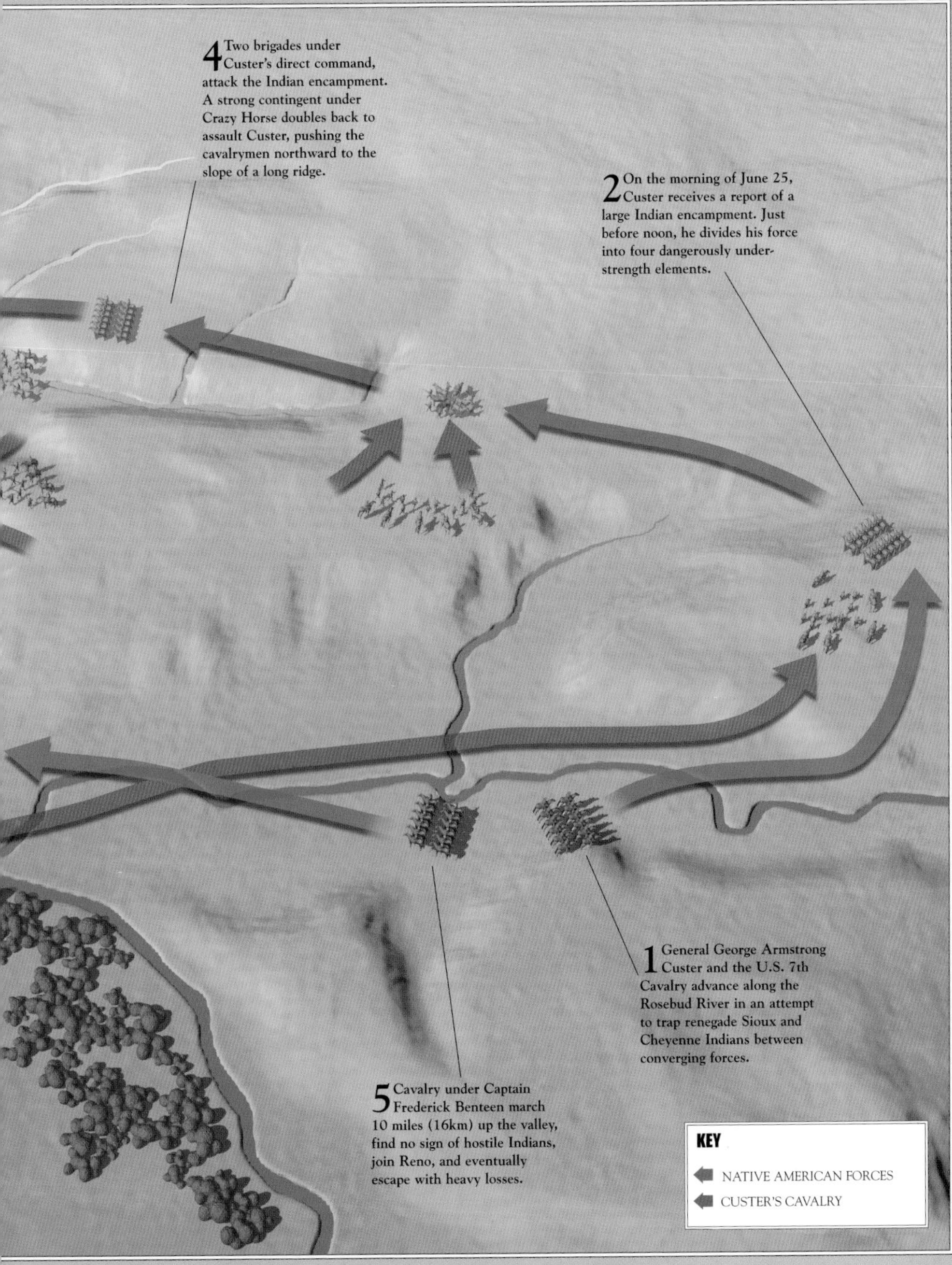

4 Two brigades under Custer's direct command, attack the Indian encampment. A strong contingent under Crazy Horse doubles back to assault Custer, pushing the cavalrymen northward to the slope of a long ridge.

2 On the morning of June 25, Custer receives a report of a large Indian encampment. Just before noon, he divides his force into four dangerously under-strength elements.

1 General George Armstrong Custer and the U.S. 7th Cavalry advance along the Rosebud River in an attempt to trap renegade Sioux and Cheyenne Indians between converging forces.

5 Cavalry under Captain Frederick Benteen march 10 miles (16km) up the valley, find no sign of hostile Indians, join Reno, and eventually escape with heavy losses.

KEY

NATIVE AMERICAN FORCES

CUSTER'S CAVALRY

ADOWA 1896

Possession of advanced firearms allowed the European colonial powers to conquer large areas in less developed regions. However, the advantage could not last forever. As the Italians found out at Adowa, motivated local troops were capable of beating colonial regulars when bearing the equivalent weaponry.

I n the nineteenth century, several European nations raced to carve out a colonial empire in Africa. Italy chose to seek sovereignty over Abyssinia (modern-day Ethiopia). There were various ways to gain control over an area. Most used a combination of economic and political influence backed up by the threat of military force. Outright conquest was another option.

It was not uncommon for a colonial power to befriend a local ruler and support him against his rivals, sometimes by supplying him with modern weapons. This was part of the Italian strategy toward Abyssinia. Rifles were supplied to arm troops loyal to the emperor in return for his friendship.

ADOWA FACTS

Who: Italian regular forces including 17,700 infantry and 56 artillery pieces under General Baratieri opposed by Abyssinian irregulars numbering up to 100,000 men armed with modern rifles, and 28 artillery pieces loyal to Emperor Menelik.

What: Dispersed Italian forces were defeated piecemeal.

Where: Near the border of Abyssinia (modern-day Ethiopia) and Eritrea.

When: March 1, 1896.

Why: Italy sought greater colonial possessions in Africa.

Outcome: Decisive defeat forced the Italian government to recognize Abyssinian independence.

LEFT: NINETEENTH-CENTURY COLONIAL WARFARE *often pitted European soldiers against large numbers of tribal irregulars. At Adowa, the irregulars were as well armed as the Europeans.*

The Italians naturally expected this arrangement to be continued when a new ruler, Emperor Menelik II (reigned 1889–1913), ascended to the throne. However, it was decided that a little duplicity was in order, just in case. The Italian government offered Menelik a treaty whereby he ceded some land in return for support. Menelik agreed and signed the dotted line, not realizing that the Italian version of the treaty was worded rather differently to the one in Amharic, the emperor's language.

A key clause in the Italian-language treaty granted Italy authority over Abyssinian dealings with foreign powers where the Amharic version simply created the provision for assistance in such dealings if it was desired. Menelik was angry when he found out he had been deliberately misled about the treaty's meaning and rejected it.

Despite the break with Italy, Menelik grew in power among the various factions in Abyssinia and was eventually proclaimed King of Kings—the first in many decades. He felt secure enough to denounce Italy, whose duplicity still stung. The Italian government was determined not to allow such a

LEFT: MENELIK II UNDERSTOOD *the potential of modern weaponry and acquired the best equipment he could for his troops. His foresight made victory at Adowa possible.*

BELOW: GENERAL BARATIERI *and other Italian officers. Baratieri was praised for his actions early in the campaign, but fell out of favor when his government decided he was being overly cautious.*

ublic challenge to go unanswered, and ordered the governor
f Italian territories in Eritrea, General Oreste Baratieri
1841–1901), to prepare a punitive expedition.

TALIAN OFFENSIVES

'unitive expeditions were a common method of suppressing
nruly colonial regions. The damage they inflicted was a
lefinite hint of what would befall if the locals did not toe the
ine, and the expedition itself served to remind everyone of
vho was in charge and just how powerful they were.

Baratieri's expedition went well, and he captured Adigrat,
Adowa, and Makalle without difficulty. It seemed as if the
talians would be able to stamp their authority on the King of
Kings in Abyssinia, as colonial overlords had done to upstart
ocal rulers in many places.

Baratieri received rewards and congratulations from the
talian government and returned to Abyssinia, intending to
apture Menelik. However, he had just 25,000 men under his
ommand with which to take on nearly 200,000 raised by the
King of Kings. About half of the Abyssinian force was armed
vith modern rifles—many of them supplied by the Italian
government in friendlier times. The Italians were forced to
all back in the face of vastly superior numbers.

A stalemate then went on for some time as supplies ran
hort for both sides. Baratieri hoped his opponent would
dvance against his positions, but Menelik sat tight until,
tung by criticism from his own government, Baratieri
aunched an attack.

Menelik was at that time encamped in Adowa, his troops
n half rations and even those running out fast. He was
onsidering a withdrawal when word came that the Italians
had sallied out with fewer than 20,000 troops and
i6 artillery pieces.

HE BATTLE OF ADOWA

Baratieri hoped to advance and occupy the high ground
round Adowa before capturing the city a second time. To
his end he divided his outnumbered force into four brigades,
each using a different route. This invited disaster at the best
of times, and with inaccurate maps movement through the
lifficult terrain was problematical. The Italian force became
adly confused, with brigades becoming intermingled, strung
ut, and outright lost during the march.

It was in this state of total confusion that an advance
orce (soon joined by an Abyssinian army numbering 100,000
nen and 28 artillery pieces) intercepted the Italian
xpedition.

In most previous "colonial" battles, the Europeans had
njoyed a massive superiority in firepower and it was not
ncommon for the locals to have only a few rifles. At Adowa,
however, there were five Abyssinian riflemen to each Italian.
Vorse, Menelik had positioned his artillery on high ground
nd the guns began pounding the Italians as they tried to

ABYSSINIAN WARRIOR

As in many other African regions, tribal
warriors of Abyssinia were simply
equipped. Wearing a white robe and armed
with a spear, they were no match for
trained regulars armed with rifles and
artillery. Numbers and raw courage could
make up some of the deficiency in
firepower, but the Europeans had come to
expect they could beat any native force.

However, many of Menelik's warriors at
Adowa were not "ill-armed savages," but
experienced, highly motivated fighters
equipped with the best rifles that Britain,
Italy, and the United States could supply.
They were even supported by their own
artillery.

reform their scattered brigades. Although the Abyssinians possessed modern firearms, theirs was not a trained European army but a vast horde of armed men led by charismatic leaders. The result was a series of uncoordinated, disorganized rushes against the Italians. This, at least, was colonial warfare the way it was supposed to be, with a recklessly courageous enemy suffering massive casualties under the disciplined fire of a professional force.

Even so, there was never any real chance that the dispersed Italians might win the battle. The Abyssinians were brave, persistent, and numerous, and if their rifle fire was inexpert and undisciplined, there was a huge amount of it. The Italians were not capable of concerted action and their forces were defeated in detail. Eventually, the surviving Italian units were able to retreat, leaving about 5,000 men dead on the field of

LEFT: ADOWA BATTLEGROUND. *The Italian army was operating in unfamiliar territory with inaccurate maps. Coordinated maneuvers were impossible.*

BELOW: A RATHER FANCIFUL DEPICTION *of the battle, giving the (correct) impression that the Abyssinians were well equipped with modern rifles and artillery.*

battle. Large numbers of men—wounded and otherwise—were captured. The Abyssinians suffered about 7,000 dead and 10,000 wounded, mainly as a result of the uncoordinated human-wave attacks they launched.

OUTCOMES

Abyssinia remained independent and gained considerable status in the international community. Those troops taken prisoner were held in Addis Ababa until the Italian government paid reparations, heaping further humiliation on the shame of defeat at the hands of local irregulars.

To some extent, changing circumstances got the better of Baratieri's expedition. Previously, small professional forces had beaten ill-armed hordes, but it was becoming possible for those hordes to obtain good, modern weaponry. The balance had shifted, and Baratieri was the victim of a failure to notice that times had changed.

However, there was more to it than that. Marching into unfamiliar territory was an occupational hazard of colonial soldiering, and doing so in the face of greater numbers was

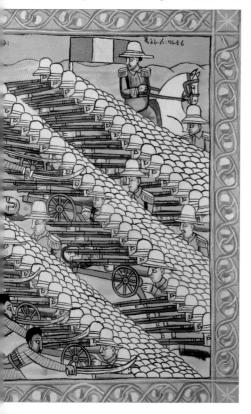

ABOVE: *THE REMNANTS OF THE ITALIAN ARMY were able to retreat to safety, leaving behind large numbers of captives in the hands of Menelik's forces.*

common practice. But Baratieri had already weighed the odds and decided they were not good. He had chosen to sit tight in a defensive position rather than boldly advance—at least until his government sent him messages calling him an incompetent coward.

In the end, then, Baratieri was goaded into advancing, against his own better judgment, by insults. Pride seems to have led him to the fateful decision to attack when, if he had waited just a week more, most of the Abyssinian army would have been sent home for lack of supplies.

ADOWA

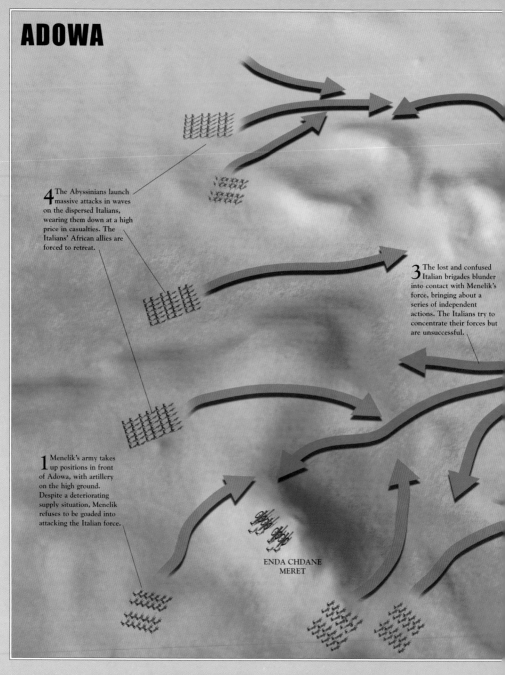

4 The Abyssinians launch massive attacks in waves on the dispersed Italians, wearing them down at a high price in casualties. The Italians' African allies are forced to retreat.

3 The lost and confused Italian brigades blunder into contact with Menelik's force, bringing about a series of independent actions. The Italians try to concentrate their forces but are unsuccessful.

1 Menelik's army takes up positions in front of Adowa, with artillery on the high ground. Despite a deteriorating supply situation, Menelik refuses to be goaded into attacking the Italian force.

ENDA CHDANE
MERET

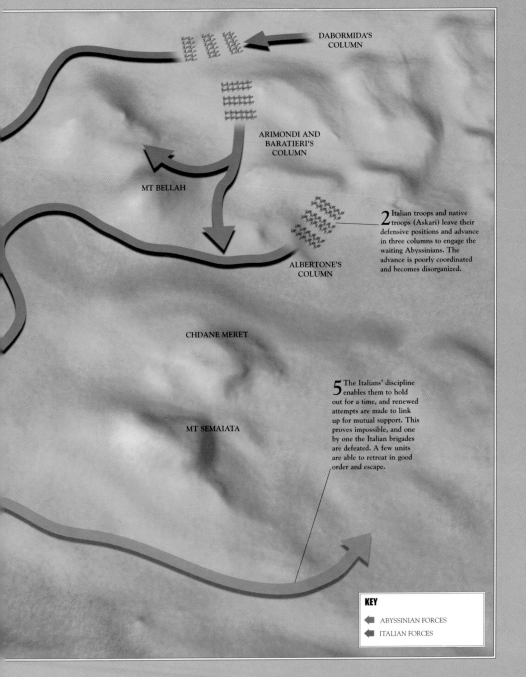

DABORMIDA'S
COLUMN

ARIMONDI AND
BARATIERI'S
COLUMN

MT BELLAH

2 Italian troops and native
troops (Askari) leave their
defensive positions and advance
in three columns to engage the
waiting Abyssinians. The
advance is poorly coordinated
and becomes disorganized.

ALBERTONE'S
COLUMN

CHDANE MERET

5 The Italians' discipline
enables them to hold
out for a time, and renewed
attempts are made to link
up for mutual support. This
proves impossible, and one
by one the Italian brigades
are defeated. A few units
are able to retreat in good
order and escape.

MT SEMAIATA

KEY

ABYSSINIAN FORCES

ITALIAN FORCES

TSUSHIMA 1905

At approximately 2:45 on the fog-shrouded morning of May 27, 1905, the Japanese merchant ship Shinano Maru *was patrolling 150 miles (240 km) south of the entrance to the Korean Straits. The ship's crew caught a glimpse of shadowy ships in the distance and knew a desperate hour had arrived. The ship's captain dashed off a wireless message: "Enemy fleet in sight in square 203. Is apparently making for the eastern channel."*

The eastern channel was named for a group of islands, Tsushima, the closest Japanese territory to the Korean peninsula. Minutes after receiving the warning, Admiral Heihachiro Togo (1848–1934) cabled the emperor in Tokyo: "I have just received news that the enemy fleet has been sighted. Our fleet will immediately put to sea to attack and destroy him."

Japan had been at war with Imperial Russia for more than a year. In January, Russia's Far East bastion at Port Arthur had capitulated following a protracted siege, and from the surrounding heights Japanese heavy guns had pounded the warships of

TSUSHIMA FACTS

Who: The Japanese fleet with 31 ships under Admiral Heihachiro Togo (1848–1934) versus the Russian Baltic Fleet with 37 ships under Admiral Zinovi Rozhestvensky (1848–1909).

What: Initially intended to join the remnants of the Russian Pacific Squadron and challenge Japanese naval supremacy, the Baltic Fleet instead attempted to reach a safe anchorage at Vladivostok.

Where: Tsushima Strait between the Japanese home island of Kyushu and the Korean peninsula.

When: May 27–28, 1905.

Why: The Japanese were determined to maintain naval preeminence in the Pacific

and hoped to strike a decisive blow against Russian prestige.

Outcome: Admiral Togo employed the classic naval maneuver of crossing the enemy's T to concentrate fire. The Russian fleet were annihilated.

LEFT: GEYSERS FROM JAPANESE SHELLFIRE *bracket the vanguard of the Russian Baltic Fleet in Tsushima Strait. The Russians held the upper hand briefly before Japanese guns were brought to bear.*

the Czar's Pacific Squadron in the harbor below into useless hulks. Before the fall of Port Arthur, Russia had renamed its Baltic Fleet the Second Pacific Squadron and committed this force to sail 18,000 nautical miles (33,336 km) in an attempt to join what remained of its navy in the East and fight the Japanese in their home waters. At first glance, the Russian Baltic Fleet was more than a match for Togo. In truth, its

prowess was suspect. Many Russian sailors were poorly trained, coerced into the service of the Czar. Many of its officers were aristocratic political appointees. Admiral Zinovy Rozhestvensky (1848–1909), commander of the Baltic Fleet, had never seen combat.

THE LONG WAY ROUND

Rozhestvensky's command weighed anchor from the port city of Reval on the Gulf of Finland on October 15, 1904. Its first division included four new battleships, *Alexander III*, *Borodino*, *Orel*, and the flagship *Suvorov*, each weighing 15,000 tons with four 12-inch (30 cm) guns and 6-inch (15 cm) secondary cannons. The modern battleship *Oslyabya* led the second division, but the quality of the remaining ships declined precipitously. Two elderly 10,000-ton battleships, *Navarin* and *Sisoi Veliky*, and the slow armored cruiser *Nakhimov* were hardly fit for battle. The remaining ships included the old battleship *Nikolai I*, and various

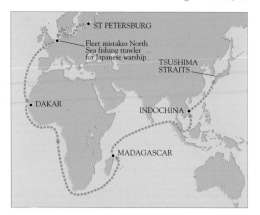

LEFT: THE RUSSIAN BALTIC FLEET sailed thousands of miles to its ill-fated rendezvous with the Imperial Japanese Navy at Tsushima. Many of the Russian warships were antiquated.

BELOW: THREE MEN SIT ON THE SHORELINE at Port Arthur while the hulks of the Russian warships Pallada *(left) and* Pobida, *shattered by Japanese artillery, rest in the harbor's mud.*

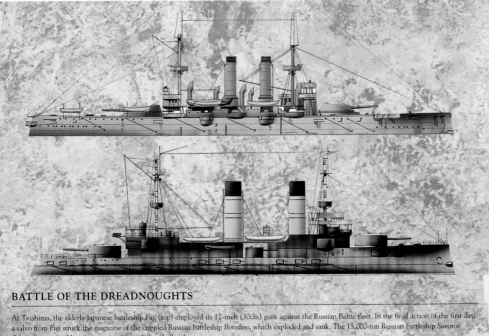

BATTLE OF THE DREADNOUGHTS

At Tsushima, the elderly Japanese battleship *Fuji* (top) employed its 12-inch (30cm) guns against the Russian Baltic fleet. In the final action of the first day, a salvo from *Fuji* struck the magazine of the crippled Russian battleship *Borodino*, which exploded and sank. The 15,000-ton Russian battleship *Suvorov* (bottom) was set ablaze from stem to stern during the battle.

cruisers and destroyers. On the eve of the Battle of Tsushima, Russian combat efficiency had seriously deteriorated during the arduous seven-month voyage.

The fleet commanded by Togo, while outnumbered, included four modern battleships. Two other battleships, *Asahi* and *Shikishima*, each of 15,500 tons with four 12-inch guns and 6-inch secondary armament, joined Togo's flagship, *Mikasa*. The older 12,500-ton battleship *Fuji* was also armed with 12-inch main batteries. At Tsushima, the Japanese employed a pair of state-of-the-art 7,700-ton armored cruisers, *Kasuga*, with a 10-inch (25 cm) gun forward and 8-inch (20 cm) guns aft, and *Nisshin*, with four 8-inch mounts. They also utilized a number of light cruisers, destroyers, and torpedo boats.

The Japanese enjoyed several advantages: They were defending home waters, and their ships were faster than their Russian adversaries. Their training, gunnery, and seamanship were superb. Russian guns were still fired manually by lanyard (attached to the firing mechanism, this cord causes a weapon to discharge when pulled), while Japanese fire control was electric, substantially improving accuracy and rate of fire. Perhaps the greatest Japanese advantage was the high level of esprit de corps in the ranks.

While anchored at Madagascar, Admiral Rozhestvensky received the disheartening news of Port Arthur's surrender. His original destination in Japanese hands, the only option was to sail for the port of Vladivostok.

THE JAPANESE NELSON

Togo weighed anchor from Masan, Korea, just before 6 A.M., on May 27. Sometime after 1 P.M., in two ragged lines, Rozhestvensky's ships emerged in Tsushima Strait. Togo signaled a message reminiscent of Lord Nelson at Trafalgar, "The fate of the empire depends upon the outcome of this battle. Let every man do his utmost duty."

Togo then took a tremendous gamble. His ships were to turn to port in succession, each executing the turn at the same position. The maneuver was dangerous because the Japanese would be exposed to Russian fire while their own guns could not reply. However, once completed, the Japanese would be crossing the Russian T, firing their heavy broadsides at the enemy against only a few of the Russians' forward guns. The Japanese sailors executed the turn with precision, but for several minutes a rain of Russian shells inflicted damage.

Mikasa turned first, and at 2:08 P.M. *Suvorov* fired a 12-inch salvo at the opposing flagship. During the first five minutes of the battle, *Mikasa* was hit a dozen times. One shell destroyed the ship's compass and bridge ladder, wounding 15 officers. The cruiser *Asama* fell out of line after taking three hits. The cruiser *Yakumo* lost her forward turret to a direct hit from *Nikolai I*.

When the Japanese ships came out of their turn, they were completely across the Russian T at a distance of 5,000 yards (4,572 m). Concentrated fire set *Suvorov* ablaze. A shell struck the flagship's bridge, wounding Rozhestvensky, who fell unconscious and was evacuated to a destroyer. *Suvorov's* helm jammed, and the doomed battleship began turning in circles. Simultaneously, *Oslyabya*, at the head of the second Russian line, capsized and sank. Following *Suvorov*, *Alexander III* began to turn in a circle with the flagship. Third in line, *Borodino* was burning furiously. During the same exchange, which reduced the *Suvorov* to a smoking ruin, *Alexander III* drifted out of control.

RELENTLESS ADMIRAL TOGO

Less than two hours later, Togo regained contact with what was left of the main Russian fleet. *Alexander III* had assumed the lead of the Russian column but rolled over and sank in a hail of Japanese fire. As *Suvorov* slipped beneath the waves, the Japanese concentrated their fire on *Borodino* and the nearby *Orel*, which was set ablaze. As daylight faded, Togo ordered his ships to disengage. Just before firing ceased, *Fuji* loosed the day's last salvo of 12-inch (30 cm) shells at the stricken *Borodino*. At least one of these penetrated the battleship's magazines, and she disappeared in a catastrophic explosion.

BELOW: ADMIRAL HEIHARICHO TOGO (1848–1934) commanded the Japanese fleet during the Battle of Tsushima from the bridge of his flagship, the battleship Mikasa.

BELOW: RUSSIAN SAILORS STRUGGLE UNDER JAPANESE FIRE as the decks of the doomed battleship Borodino *are awash. The stricken vessel sank moments later.*

ABOVE: *THE RESOUNDING VICTORY OVER THE RUSSIANS at Tsushima touched off celebrations across Japan and energized a wave of nationalistic fervor.*

Command of the shattered Russian fleet devolved to Admiral Nikolai Nebogatov (1849–1922) aboard *Nikolai I*. In a vain attempt to resume a course for Vladivostok, Nebogatov ordered his fleet to take a northerly course. In the darkness, Japanese torpedo boats and destroyers attacked. The *Sisoi Veliky* took a torpedo aft and sank about daylight, while four torpedoes smashed into *Navarin*, which went down at 10 P.M.

The Russian cruisers that accompanied the main body were decimated. *Svetlana* was cornered by three Japanese cruisers the next day and sunk with no survivors. *Nakhimov* and *Monomakh* were damaged and scuttled, and the old cruiser *Dmitri Donskoi* also went down.

On the morning of May 28, Nebogatov found he was hemmed in on three sides by Japanese cruisers and Togo's main force again moving across the Russian T. The Japanese stood out of range of the most powerful remaining Russian guns and began shelling the survivors from 12,000 yards (11,000 m). Nebogatov ordered his flag lowered to half-mast and sought surrender terms. Only the cruiser *Izumrud* and two destroyers reached Vladivostok. Rozhestvensky was taken prisoner.

OUTCOME

Tsushima had been a debacle for the Russians. They had lost 34 ships, 4,830 dead, and 5,917 wounded and captured. The Japanese lost only three torpedo boats. Several ships were damaged, with 110 killed and 590 wounded.

Japan's victory over a traditional European power stunned the world. President Theodore Roosevelt (1858–1919) offered to mediate peace talks, and the Treaty of Portsmouth, which included major territorial concessions from Russia, ended the Russo-Japanese War on September 5, 1905.

TSUSHIMA

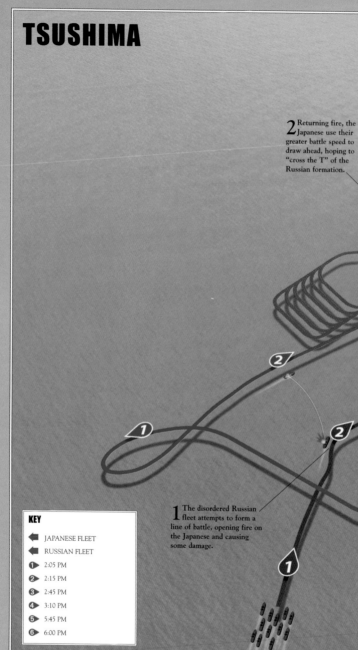

2 Returning fire, the Japanese use their greater battle speed to draw ahead, hoping to "cross the T" of the Russian formation.

1 The disordered Russian fleet attempts to form a line of battle, opening fire on the Japanese and causing some damage.

3 The flagships of the first and second Russian divisions both suffer heavy damage. *Oslyabya* sinks; *Suvarov* is driven out of the battle line.

KEY

◀	JAPANESE FLEET
◀	RUSSIAN FLEET
❶▶	2:05 PM
❷▶	2:15 PM
❸▶	2:45 PM
❹▶	3:10 PM
❺▶	5:45 PM
❻▶	6:00 PM

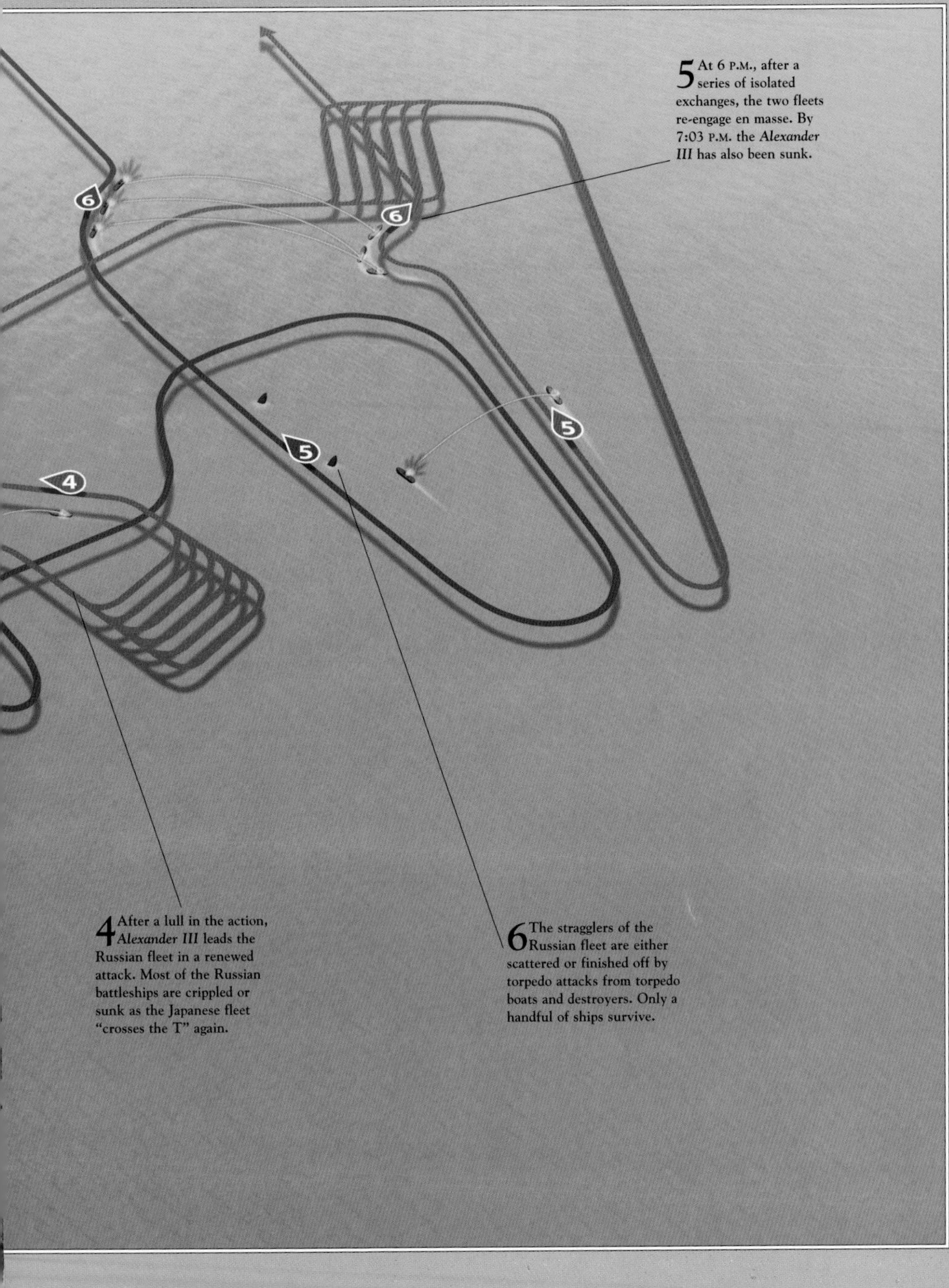

5 At 6 P.M., after a series of isolated exchanges, the two fleets re-engage en masse. By 7:03 P.M. the *Alexander III* has also been sunk.

4 After a lull in the action, *Alexander III* leads the Russian fleet in a renewed attack. Most of the Russian battleships are crippled or sunk as the Japanese fleet "crosses the T" again.

6 The stragglers of the Russian fleet are either scattered or finished off by torpedo attacks from torpedo boats and destroyers. Only a handful of ships survive.

Gallipoli lies chiefly in the disregard of Allied commanders for the difficulty of the task assigned to their troops—a task that heroism alone could not successfully complete.

WHY GALLIPOLI?

Opposing static lines separated by a bleak no-man's land characterized the stalemate of the Western Front in World War I and left military planners of both the Allied a[nd] Central Powers searching for an alternative that might le[ad] to ultimate victory. Responding to a plea from their Russi[an] allies, the British and French settled on an attempt to se[ize] the Dardanelles, a narrow waterway connecting the Black [Sea] to the Mediterranean. Control of this strait would establis[h a] supply line to Russia, relieve pressure on the Czar's Easte[rn] Front armies, and possibly compel Turkey, which had enter[ed] the war on the side of the Central Powers in October, 19[14,] to sue for peace.

Initially, it was believed that the Dardanelles might [be] secured and even the Turkish capital at Constantino[ple] captured with the use of naval forces alone. However, it w[as] soon discovered that land troops would have to secure t[he] heights that commanded either side of the Dardanelles [in] order for shipping to transit the waterway unscathe[d.] Eventually, the Allies committed more than 400,0[00] soldiers to the land expedition, while the Turks deploy[ed] about half a million. Among the principal advocates of t[he] Gallipoli operation were Churchill and Lord Herbe[rt] Kitchener (1850–1916), British Secretary of State for W[ar.] The disaster in the Dardanelles would prove a serious blow [to] the reputations of these statesmen, as well as the death kne[ll] of the careers of several Allied field commanders.

NAVAL FIASCO

On February 19, 1915, a flotilla of 42 Allied warship[s,] including the new battleship *Queen Elizabeth* mountin[g] 15-inch (38 cm) main batteries, pounded Turkish fortificatio[ns] in the Dardanelles but achieved limited results. A mont[h] later, a fleet of 18 battleships, many of them obsolete, alon[g] with numerous cruisers and destroyers, attempted to run th[e] gauntlet of Turkish guns and floating mines. Near th[e] narrowest part of the strait, scarcely a mile wide, th[e] battleships HMS *Irresistible* and HMS *Ocean* were sunk, an[d] the battleship HMS *Inflexible* seriously damaged. The Frenc[h] battleship *Bouvet* exploded and sank, while two other[s,] *Suffren* and *Gaulois*, were heavily damaged.

HELLES AND ANZAC COVE

When it became apparent that naval power alone could no[t] secure the Dardanelles, a plan was devised to lan[d] Commonwealth and French troops on the peninsula o[f] Gallipoli with the intent that they advance rapidly overlan[d] and capture the Turkish fortifications. The Allied forc[e] consisted of the British 29th Division, the Royal Nava[l] Division, the Australian and New Zealand Army Corp[s] (ANZAC), and the French Oriental Expeditionary Corp[s.] The ANZAC troops had been in Egypt training for the Western Front. Their diversion to the Dardanelles and the marshaling of troops from Europe allowed the Turks preciou[s] time to reinforce their defenses along the heights near the water's edge. On April 25, British and French troops came

ANZAC SOLDIER

Along with British and French troops, the bulk of the Allied soldiers at Gallipoli were ANZACS, members of the Australia and New Zealand Army Corps. This ANZAC soldier carries the standard issue Lee-Enfield .303 rifle with bayonet fixed and wears a jaunty Bush-style hat. The fighting at Gallipoli helped forge the national identities of Australia and New Zealand.

ABOVE: TURKISH TROOPS FOUGHT GALLANTLY *and suffered great privations at Gallipoli. Among them was Mustafa Kemal, the father of modern Turkey.*

LEFT: DUGOUTS, SUCH AS THIS ONE AT HELLES, *provided shelter and some protection against enemy artillery and snipers, although they also became home to vermin of every description.*

ashore at Helles, on the southern end of the Gallipoli peninsula, while ANZAC troops disembarked near Gaba Tepe on the coast of the Aegean Sea. The operation continually suffered from inadequate planning and tactical execution. Amphibious landings under fire from hostile forces, which occupied surrounding high ground, had rarely taken place.

At Helles, the old collier *River Clyde*, converted to a troop transport, was run aground to land its soldiers. The men of the Royal Hampshires and the Royal Munster Fusiliers stepped down narrow gangways into a hail of machine-gun fire. Only 21 of the initial 200 men off the ship managed to reach the shore unscathed. The Lancashire Fusiliers lost 600 of their 1,000 men in the first hours of battle. ANZAC forces also sustained heavy casualties north of Gaba Tepe, and their confined landing area has come to be known as ANZAC Cove.

Throughout the spring of 1915, attempts to penetrate the Turkish cordon and capture the town of Krithia failed.

Turkish forces, commanded by German General Otto Liman von Sanders (1855–1929), were too weak to push the invaders into the sea. While the thinly stretched Turkish lines staved off appreciable Allied gains, counterattacks were fruitless.

BRUTAL ATTRITION

Indicative of the high casualties suffered were the ANZAC assault on May 2–3 against Baby 700, the smaller of two hills that dominated their exposed positions at ANZAC Cove, and the Turkish offensive against ANZAC Cove on May 19. Within hours of attacking, ANZAC troops were forced to retreat, having suffered hundreds of casualties traversing gullies and ravines against murderous fire. When more than

ABOVE: BRITISH TROOPS, NEWLY ARRIVED AT GALLIPOLI, advance resolutely uphill. Machine-gun fire took a heavy toll on advancing troops of both sides.

40,000 Turkish soldiers hit an ANZAC force less than half of their size, the attackers lost 10,000 casualties.

On August 6, Allied troops landed at Suvla Bay, intending to link up with forces at ANZAC Cove. Within a week primarily due to the ineptitude of field commanders, the attack lost momentum. Thus, a third Allied lodgment was effectively bottled up.

After months of fighting, the lines at Gallipoli began to resemble those of the Western Front. Snipers picked off soldiers who raised their heads above the trenches. Unburied

ABOVE: *TURKISH GUNNERS pose next to a massive siege gun, the Dardanelles, 1915. Artillery played a major role in ensuring Allied troops never broke out of their beach heads.*

corpses bloated in the stifling heat of summer, and clouds of flies compounded the misery. Fall and winter brought rain, snow, and freezing temperatures. Turkish artillery dominated Allied positions, and the troops were constantly subjected to shelling. When Hamilton requested nearly 100,000 additional soldiers for Gallipoli at the end of August, he received only one-quarter of that number.

With their hopes for a decisive victory in the Dardanelles dashed, discord was rife among Allied leaders. By October, confidence in Hamilton's leadership had evaporated. At long last, on December 7, more than 100,000 men were evacuated from ANZAC Cove. The withdrawal of 35,000 soldiers from Helles did not occur until January 9, 1916.

EPILOGUE

An investigation into the debacle produced a report in 1919 that failed to censure any prominent political or military leaders. Nevertheless, Gallipoli stained the reputations of Lord Kitchener, General Hamilton, and numerous other prominent figures. Most notable among these was Churchill, who resigned after admitting the failure of the naval operations. A quarter of a century later, however, he rose like the mythical phoenix to guide his nation through the turbulent years of World War II. Among the Turkish military leaders at Gallipoli was Mustafa Kemal (1881–1938),

ABOVE: *LORD HERBERT KITCHENER, British Secretary of State for War, visits the front lines at Gallipoli. The costly stalemate damaged Kitchener's reputation.*

a young lieutenant colonel who rose rapidly to prominence. Kemal was later instrumental in the establishment of the Turkish Republic and gained the title of Atatürk, or Father of the Turks.

Historians assert that the national identities of Australia and New Zealand were forged in the crucible of Gallipoli. Each year, April 25 is observed in both countries as ANZAC Day.

GALLIPOLI

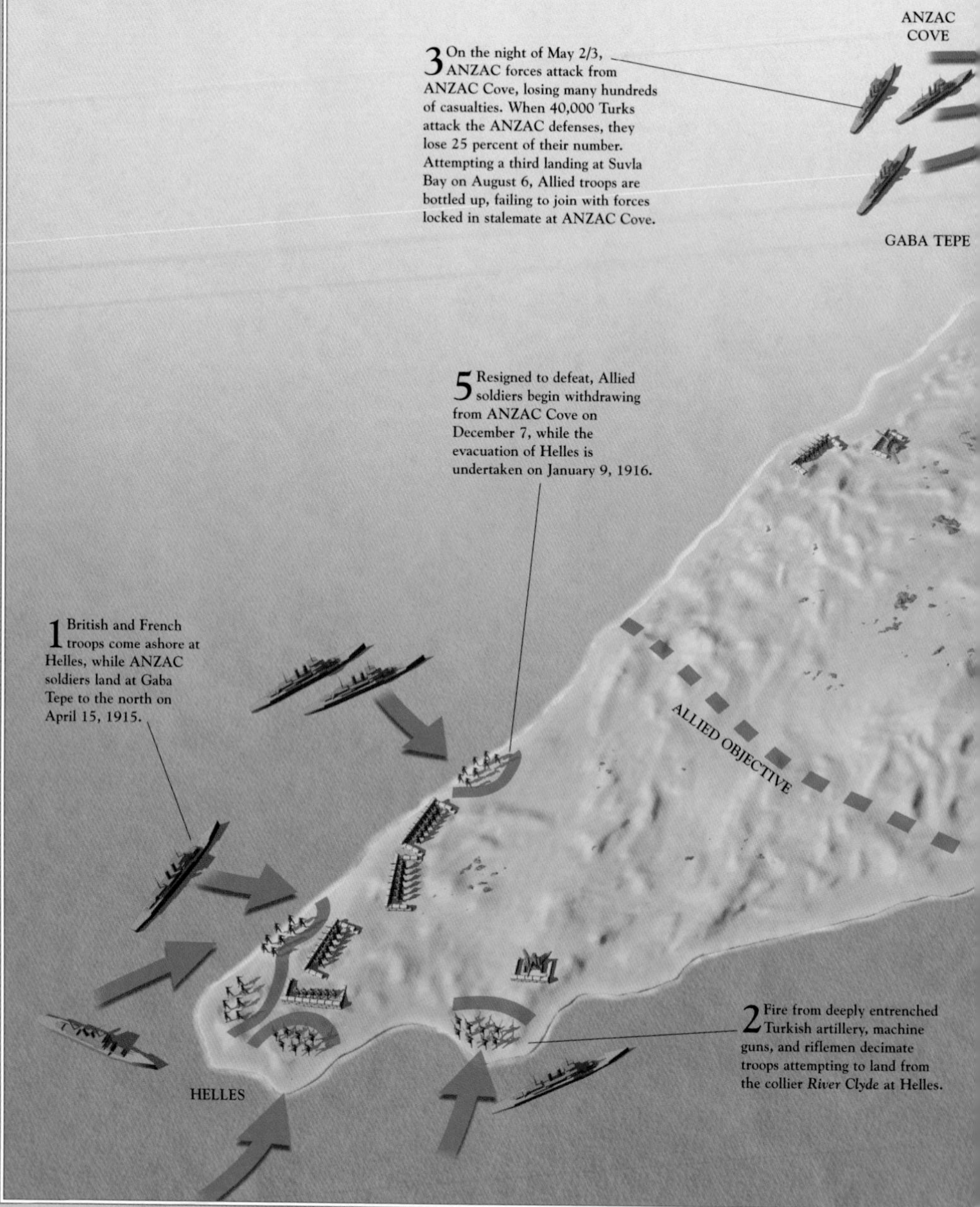

ANZAC
COVE

3 On the night of May 2/3, ANZAC forces attack from ANZAC Cove, losing many hundreds of casualties. When 40,000 Turks attack the ANZAC defenses, they lose 25 percent of their number. Attempting a third landing at Suvla Bay on August 6, Allied troops are bottled up, failing to join with forces locked in stalemate at ANZAC Cove.

GABA TEPE

5 Resigned to defeat, Allied soldiers begin withdrawing from ANZAC Cove on December 7, while the evacuation of Helles is undertaken on January 9, 1916.

1 British and French troops come ashore at Helles, while ANZAC soldiers land at Gaba Tepe to the north on April 15, 1915.

ALLIED OBJECTIVE

2 Fire from deeply entrenched Turkish artillery, machine guns, and riflemen decimate troops attempting to land from the collier *River Clyde* at Helles.

HELLES

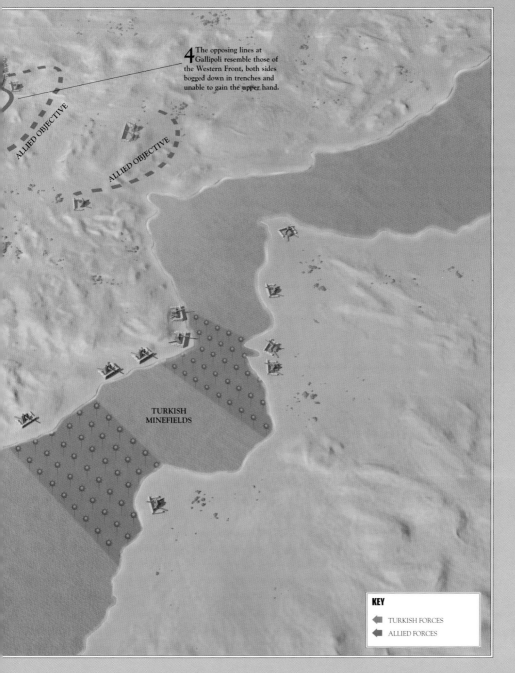

4 The opposing lines at
Gallipoli resemble those of
the Western Front, both sides
bogged down in trenches and
unable to gain the upper hand.

ALLIED OBJECTIVE

ALLIED OBJECTIVE

TURKISH
MINEFIELDS

KEY

TURKISH FORCES

ALLIED FORCES

CAPORETTO 1917

During World War I, the horror of trench warfare on the Western Front was like nothing that senior commanders of either the Allied or Central Powers could have imagined. The static lines of opposing armies stretched from the North Sea to the Swiss frontier, changing little as offensive operations ebbed and flowed.

S talemate, however, was not only to be found in the West. To the south, where the Italian army faced the forces of Austria-Hungary on a 400-mile (644 km) front, neither could gain the upper hand in the only logical area for offensive operations, the Isonzo River Valley. Italy had entered the war on May 23, 1915, and its war planners had long conceived of a bold move into Austria-Hungary through the Isonzo Valley. Perhaps, should it meet with success, the Italian army could drive northward—even to the gates of Vienna.

The advantage, however, obviously lay with the defenders. For more than 60 miles (96 km), the Isonzo flowed through Austria-Hungary parallel to the Italian border. On either side rose high mountains, stretching from Alpine passes to the

CAPORETTO FACTS

Who: General Luigi Cadorna and an Italian army of 41 divisions versus a combined German and Austro-Hungarian army of 35 divisions under General Otto von Below.

What: German and Austro-Hungarian forces conducted a deftly executed offensive against poorly prepared Italian defenses.

Where: Near the town of Caporetto in modern-day Slovenia.

When: October 24–November 9, 1917.

Why: The Central Powers assumed the offensive to relieve pressure on the forces of Austria-Hungary.

Outcome: Italian forces were routed in a defeat of epic proportions. Italian losses were enormous: 11,000 were killed, 20,000 wounded, and 265,000 were taken prisoner.

LEFT: *ITALIAN TROOPS RETREAT in disorder along the Udine-Codroisto road following their decisive defeat at Caporetto.*

Adriatic Sea, and the river was prone to flooding during heavy rains. The challenge for Italian General Luigi Cadorna (1850–1928) was formidable. To transit the valley, enemy troops defending the mountains on either flank must be dislodged.

THE FUTILE FRONT

For two years, the Italians attempted to wrest control of the Isonzo Valley from the Austro-Hungarians. No fewer than 11 times did Cadorna assault the enemy defenses. The campaign collectively known as the Fourth Battle of the Isonzo, from November 10 to December 2, 1915, was indicative of the frustrating and costly combat that took place. During three weeks of desperate fighting, the Italians failed to capture any significant objectives or substantial territory. The Austro-Hungarian stronghold at Mount Sei Busi was assaulted five times to no avail. Each side was being bled white. The Italians lost nearly 50,000 dead and wounded, while the Austro-Hungarians, already stretched to the breaking point along their thinly held front, suffered 32,000

casualties. For the first time, their grimly resolute commander, General Conrad von Hotzendorf (1852–1925), appealed to his German allies for assistance. Although the Germans were sympathetic, they were not yet officially at war with Italy, and the request was declined.

BRINK OF DISASTER

The worst, however, was yet to come. The war of attrition dragged on for months. Casualties on both sides rose into the hundreds of thousands. Cadorna's eleventh offensive, launched August 17, 1917, pushed the Austro-Hungarians to the limit of their endurance. General Luigi Capello (1859–1941) and the Italian Second Army had seized the strategically vital Bainsizza Plateau and threatened to unhinge the entire front. Finally, their losses so great that they feared they could hold no longer, the Austro-Hungarians made a last desperate plea for assistance to Berlin.

BELOW: WOUNDED AUSTRIAN SOLDIERS AWAIT MEDICAL ATTENTION at a field hospital. The numerous attacks and counterattacks at Caporetto claimed thousands of casualties.

This time, aware that an Austro-Hungarian collapse would oblige him to fight on the southern front regardless, General Erich Ludendorff (1865–1937), chief strategist of the German General Staff, relented and dispatched six divisions to aid his co-belligerents. When the German troops arrived at the Isonzo, the situation changed. The Battle of Caporetto, also known as the Twelfth Battle of the Isonzo, would prove to be a dramatic reversal of fortune.

THE DEFENSIVE OFFENSIVE

From time to time, military planners have reached the conclusion that the most effective defensive posture lies in assuming the offensive. Such was the case at Caporetto. Among the German troops who ventured south was General Konrad Kraft von Dellmensingen (1862–1953), an acknowledged expert in mountain warfare. Surveying the terrain, Dellmensingen proposed an attack against the Italians, whom he suspected would be ill prepared. Ludendorff assented, accepting that tremendous risk accompanied the plan. Failure could mean a general collapse along the entire line, while the precious German divisions diverted from other fronts were irreplaceable.

Boldly conceived, the fall offensive was to be a coordinated effort. Two Austrian armies, commanded by General Svetozar Borojevic (1856–1920), were to assault Italian positions on the east side of the salient they occupied on the hard-won Bainsizza Plateau. The newly constituted Fourteenth Army, which included the six fresh German divisions and nine Austrian divisions led by German General Otto von Below (1857–1944), were to strike the northeastern shoulder of the salient from the nearby Alps. Counting on speed and the

ABOVE: GENERAL LUIGI CADORNA *commanded Italian troops in the Isonzo River Valley during numerous abortive offensive efforts against thoroughly entrenched Austro-Hungarian forces.*

SKODA 75MM MOUNTAIN GUN M1915

The Skoda 75mm (3in) Mountain Gun M1915 resulted from a concerted effort by the Czech arms manufacturer to develop artillery that could be disassembled rapidly, transported by mules into the mountains, and placed in action. The weapon proved successful and became a mainstay of the Austro-Hungarian forces during World War I. It was widely used during the fighting around Caporetto.

ABOVE: AUSTRIAN ARTILLERYMEN, bundled against the severe winter weather in the rugged mountains near Caporetto, prepare to go into action against Italian positions.

RIGHT: GERMAN TROOPS ADVANCE TOWARD the front at Caporetto. Their assault at Caporetto resulted in a calamity for the defending Italian troops.

element of surprise, the attack could possibly restore the original line, at least returning the front to the status quo. In the center of the two-pronged thrust lay the village of Caporetto.

OUT OF THE MIST

At 2 A.M. on October 24, 1917, the predawn stillness was shattered by the thunder of German and Austro-Hungarian artillery. Caught unawares, the Italians were exposed to a murderous hail of gas and high-explosive shells. During the four-hour bombardment, many Italian soldiers discovered, to their horror, that their gas masks were ineffective in filtering the deadly chemicals released by the enemy.

Among the German troops who had recently arrived were a relative few specially trained soldiers whose role was to infiltrate enemy trenches. Armed with rifles and hand grenades, these shock troops (which came to be known as storm troopers), usually moved forward in squad strength under a creeping artillery barrage. Striking positions identified as the weakest along the opposing line, they avoided pitched combat when possible, disrupting communications, seizing command posts, and spreading confusion. At Caporetto, effective artillery bombardment and storm-trooper operations compounded the poor Italian defensive preparedness.

The morning mist and smoke from the artillery fire shrouded the battlefield as the main German and Austro-Hungarian assaults stepped off about 6:30 A.M. Those Italian troops still manning forward positions spotted the silhouettes but were unable to immediately identify the soldiers coming toward them. Numerous Italian frontline positions were quickly overrun.

Chaos reigned as Italian soldiers were shot down in their trenches, raised their hands in surrender, or threw their weapons to the ground and fled toward the rear. On the first day, the Germans and Austro-Hungarians penetrated 14 miles (22 km). Within the week, they had occupied Udine, where Cadorna had previously been headquartered. By the end of the month, they had reached the Tagliamonte River, halting only when they had advanced an astonishing 70 miles (113 km), their supply lines stretched and mobility hindered by heavy rain and a lack of motorized transportation. Cadorna's center collapsed, and he withdrew rapidly, finally halting in early November along the banks of the Piave River, less than 20 miles (32 km) from Venice. Great Britain and France both diverted troops from other fronts to shore up the Italians.

The offensive had exceeded the grandest expectations of its commanders. Italian losses were at least 11,000 killed, 20,000 wounded, and 275,000 captured, although some estimates of the number taken prisoner exceed a staggering 500,000. German losses totaled about 20,000 dead and wounded. Cadorna was sacked and replaced by General Armando Diaz (1861–1928), who was given the task of rebuilding a shattered army. During the fighting, Erwin Rommel (1891–1944), a young lieutenant commanding a company of mountain troops, earned the Pour le Mérite, one of Germany's highest military decorations, for his part in the capture of Monte Matajur

RIGHT: GERMAN STORM TROOPERS look over the parapet of trenches in the Caporetto region. Storm troopers proved very effective in exploiting weaknesses in the Italian lines.

and 3,000 Italian soldiers. One-quarter century later during World War II, Rommel gained fame as the Desert Fox, commanding the vaunted *Afrika Korps*.

EPILOGUE

While the victory of the Central Powers at Caporetto was nothing short of spectacular, one major development did benefit the Allied cause. The disaster led to the Rapallo Conference, establishing the Supreme War Council to facilitate unity of command and cooperation between the Allied armies. For years to come, the world "Caporetto" itself was familiar in the Italian lexicon, synonymous with catastrophic defeat.

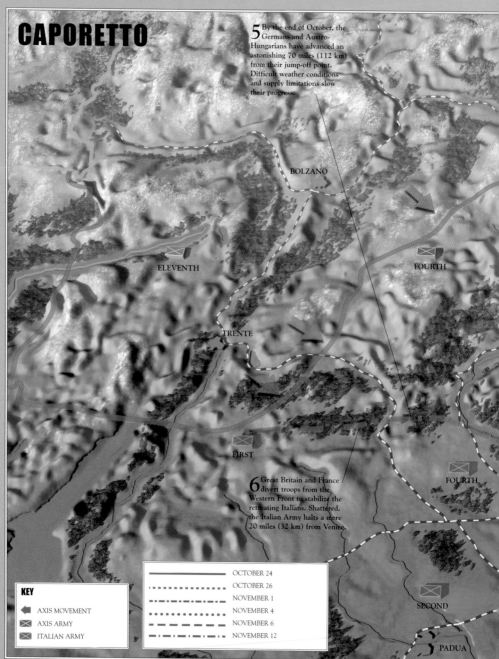

CAPORETTO

5 By the end of October, the Germans and Austro-Hungarians have advanced an astonishing 70 miles (112 km) from their jump-off point. Difficult weather conditions and supply limitations slow their progress.

BOLZANO

ELEVENTH

FOURTH

TRENTE

FIRST

FOURTH

6 Great Britain and France divert troops from the Western Front to stabilize the retreating Italians. Shattered, the Italian Army halts a mere 20 miles (32 km) from Venice.

	OCTOBER 24
	OCTOBER 26
	NOVEMBER 1
	NOVEMBER 4
	NOVEMBER 6
	NOVEMBER 12

KEY

AXIS MOVEMENT

AXIS ARMY

ITALIAN ARMY

SECOND

PADUA

2 On October 24, 1917, bolstered by six German divisions, the Austro-Hungarians launch attacks against Italian positions along a broad front. A preparatory artillery bombardment wreaks havoc among the Italians.

1 Following two years of stalemate in the mountains along the Italian front, the German high command responds to pleas for assistance, sending troops to the aid of Austria-Hungary.

TENTH

FOURTEENTH

SECOND

FIRST

UDINE

SECOND

THIRD

TREVISO

THIRD

TRIESTE

3 Specially trained to infiltrate enemy lines, German shock troops, known as storm troopers, exploit initial successes and spread confusion among the frontline Italian units.

4 On the first day of the offensive, German and Austro-Hungarian forces penetrate the Italian lines up to 14 miles (22.5 km). Only the difficult terrain and darkness halt their advance.

VENICE

PEARL HARBOR 1941

With its assault in December 1941 on the Hawaiian naval base at Pearl Harbor, Japan intended to destroy U.S. might in the Pacific. Despite successive warnings from allied intelligence and mounting tension on both sides, American commanders were totally unprepared. The result was the immolation of their battleship force.

O n the morning of Sunday, December 7, 1941, at Pearl Harbor, Lieutenant William W. Outerbridge (1906–86), of the destroyer U.S.S. *Ward* spotted the conning tower of a small submarine. It was approaching the channel leading to Pearl's main anchorage, out of bounds to U.S. craft. From the bridge, Outerbridge gave the order to open fire.

At 6:45 a.m., a shell ripped into the conning tower and the submarine vanished. Around the same time, 1,000 miles (1,600 km) to the northeast, torpedoes smashed into the hull of the U.S. freighter *Cynthia Olsen*, whose radio operator tapped out a message that an unidentified submarine was attacking.

PEARL HARBOR FACTS

Who The Imperial Japanese Navy versus the U.S. Navy. Captain Mitsuo Fuchida led the first wave of an attack of 183 aircraft. Rear Admiral Shigekazu Shimazaki led the second wave of 171 planes.

What: A surprise attack by Japanese carrier-based aircraft on the main U.S. naval base in the Pacific, within U.S. territory.

Where: Pearl Harbor, situated on the Hawaiian island of Oahu.

When: December 7, 1941

Why: The aim was to destroy the U.S. Pacific fleet and build up a defensive rim of air and naval bases around the central and southwestern Pacific.

Outcome: The attack destroyed much of the American Pacific Fleet and brought the United States into World War II.

JAPAN

PEARL HARBOR ✠

Pacific Ocean

LEFT: IN A LIGHTNING STRIKE shortly before 8 A.M. on Sunday December 7, 1941, Japanese aircraft attacked the U.S. Navy fleet anchored at Pearl Harbor. Here, U.S. Navy firefighters attempt to put out flames on board the battleship U.S.S. West Virginia.

155

These two incidents prefaced an attack on Pearl Harbor, the threat of which the Americans had been utterly unaware. U.S. President Franklin D. Roosevelt (1882–1945) and American Pacific Fleet commander-in-chief Admiral Husband E. Kimmel (1882–1968) had believed that the Japanese would strike British and Dutch positions first, and possibly U.S. bases in the Philippines.

"DON'T WORRY ABOUT IT"

The 96 warships in harbor at Pearl that Sunday were unmanned, with most of their crews off duty. Kimmel was playing golf. Yet there had been ominous signs. On the northern tip of Oahu, Lieutenant Kermit Tyler, the station's duty officer, received reports of unexplained blips on the radar screen. Believing that these were an expected flight of American B-17 bombers, Tyler declared: "Don't worry about it," dismissing the possibility that they could be hostile Japanese aircraft. Yet 30 minutes later American ships were being bombed. Tyler's miscalculation, combined with earlier delays by Washington intelligence, meant that the last chance of countering a Japanese attack had been lost.

Mastermind of the offensive was Admiral Isoruku Yamamoto (1854–1943), Japanese Combined Fleet Commander-in-Chief. A cool realist, Yamamoto was well

ABOVE: A JAPANESE AIRCRAFT CARRIER sizes up for the Pearl Harbor attack. Carriers are a vital arm of the Pearl Harbor Striking Force, including fast battleships, cruisers, and destroyers, with tankers to fuel the ships.

aware that in a lengthy conflict Japan could not hope to beat the United States with its superior industrial and armed strength. Japan therefore had never intended an official declaration of war. Instead it delivered one swift blow to destroy U.S. power in the Pacific, moving in on Pearl Harbor with 350 aircraft from six carriers, together with midget submarines. The Japanese naval task force included six aircraft carriers and the strike force comprised two fleet carriers, two converted carriers, two light carriers and two battleships along with cruisers, destroyers, and support ships.

SURPRISE IS VITAL

Yamamoto believed that after an exhausting campaign Roosevelt would be forced into a negotiated peace, but the element of surprise was vital. The carrier striking force of Vice Admiral Chuichi Nagumo (1887–1944), setting sail from the Kuril Islands off northeastern Japan, made for the attack's launching point north of Oahu. Japanese envoys in Washington had already been instructed to continue mokescreen negotiations about a possible Japanese withdrawal up to the last possible moment. Additionally, as a deliberate distraction, the Japanese luxury liner *Tatsuma Maru* had been sent on what was purported to be a 12-day voyage to San Francisco. Washington, totally oblivious to Japan's true intentions, reasoned that any possible hostilities would be unlikely to start before the ship's return to Japan. The trap was set—the liner would turn around at the vital moment and make full speed for Yokohama.

ATTACK COMMENCES

Japanese aircraft swooped down on Pearl Harbor at 7:50 a.m. With the start of the attack, one of Japan's most experienced naval aviators, Mitsuo Fuchida (1902–1976), and his crew sent the pre-arranged signal: "Tora! Tora! Tora!" ("Tiger! Tiger! Tiger!") to Nagumo. Four of the U.S. battleships were blown out of the water, four others damaged, and 11 warships sunk or disabled. Casualties mounted as the attackers turned to the airfields, destroying 188 aircraft on the ground. By the end of the day, of nine American battleships capable of offensive or defensive action, only two were fit to enter combat. Japan's battleships commanded the Pacific.

At his home on a hill overlooking the harbor, Kimmel, totally unsuspecting, was on the phone to fleet duty officer, Commander Vincent Murphy (1896–1974), who suddenly

RIGHT: A U.S. MARINE *stands guard on one of the many U.S. Navy bases scattered across the Pacific. He is armed with a Springfield rifle and has a gas-mask container slung from his left shoulder.*

broke off to read him a dispatch. It said: "The Japanese are attacking Pearl Harbor, and this is no drill." Equally unprepared was Hawaii's army commander Lieutenant General Walter Campbell Short (1880–1949). He had largely disregarded reconnaissance and radar reports, and, to make matters worse, had ordered his aircraft to be parked in the center of airfields, where, wing tip to wing tip, they offered a perfect target to Japan's aerial barrages.

Elsewhere, several warnings had been inexplicably ignored. Aboard a Honolulu-bound cruise liner, SS *Lurline*, a radio operator had detected low-frequency signals northwest of Hawaii, also noted by an intelligence officer in San Francisco. Equally serious, Dutch intelligence had intercepted and decoded a message from Tokyo to the Japanese ambassador in Bangkok, alerting him that Malaya, the Philippines, and Hawaii were likely to be attacked. The Dutch duly warned U.S. authorities, yet no action was taken.

ANTI-AIRCRAFT FIRE

At this time, Zeros, Japanese combat aircraft, totally outclassed all Allied fighters and had an added advantage of

LEFT: NEWS OF THE RAID—*the "day of infamy"—came as a thunderbolt to the United States. The fury is reflected in stark media coverage.*

being virtually impervious to antiaircraft guns. But defense forces on the ground began to rally. Soon, a knot of undamaged guns were sending their shells skyward. However, B17 bombers flying in from California, along with aircraft from the carrier U.S.S. *Enterprise* to the south, ran into a merciless Japanese barrage. A second wave of attackers arrowed in over the eastern coast, aiming at a key naval station. But the Americans on the ground were ready for them. Increasing ground fire worried Nagumo, who had failed to destroy the shore installations, most notably the oil storage bunkers that would have put the American Pacific Fleet out of action. As well, three U.S. carriers of the Pacific fleet were unaccounted for at the time. It was therefore decided not to renew the attack.

A DATE WHICH WILL LIVE IN INFAMY

In the U.S., news of the raid was greeted first with stunned disbelief, then boiling anger. The day after the invasion, President Roosevelt addressed Congress and the Supreme Court, asking Congress to declare war on Japan to avenge the previous day, "a date," he said, "which will live in infamy." Germany and Italy had been unaware of their ally Japan's move to attack but supported it, declaring war on the United States on December 11. As for those held responsible for the Pearl Harbor debacle, Husband Kimmel, despite more than 30 years of naval service, was dismissed 10 days

BELOW: TAKEN FROM A JAPANESE AIRCRAFT, *this photograph shows U.S. Navy battleships lined up at "Battleship Row." The lines of torpedoes cutting through the water can be seen heading towards the anchored ships.*

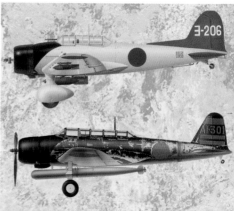

JAPANESE BOMBERS

Although the elliptical-winged Aichi D3A (Allied code name "Val," *see top*) became the standard Japanese carrier-based aircraft, the first prototype, completed in December 1937, proved disappointing in trials. However, in the early phases, the aircraft had an outstanding role in spearheading the attack on Pearl Harbor. The D3A remained a serious menace but by 1943 it was up against heavily defended ships and better Allied fighters, and so was downgraded to second line and kamikaze service. The Nakajima B5N "Kate" (*see lower image*) was used mainly as carrier-borne torpedo bomber, and had great success in the early years of the war. B5Ns fought at most of the major sea battles in the Pacific.

ABOVE: *THE U.S.S. WEST VIRGINIA was struck by up to nine enemy torpedoes, and more than 100 of her officers and men were killed.*

RIGHT: *BOMBED AND STRAFED BY THE JAPANESE, Hickam Field suffered extensive damage and aircraft losses, with 189 killed and 303 wounded.*

after the raid for disregarding intelligence received from Washington, persisting in his belief that the Philippines were the first likely target. Campbell Short suffered the same fate. In January 1942, a supreme court found both men guilty of dereliction of duty. A later investigation by Congress proved more lenient, however, declaring both men had made errors of judgment.

AFTERMATH

Pearl Harbor was intended to smash both America's means of retaliation and her resolution. Both aims failed. Of the vessels damaged, all but two were salvaged, and many crews were saved. Shore installations remained mostly undamaged. The violation of U.S. territory served only to unite the nation. A year later, Japan's first defeat on land at Guadalcanal (August 1942 – January 1943) began the Allies' Pacific comeback.

PEARL HARBOR

6 The U.S.S. *Nevada*, attacked by torpedoes and divebombers, suffers 60 killed and 190 wounded. It forces down some Japanese aircraft before sinking.

FORD ISLAND NAVAL
AIR STATION

US NAVY
YARD

5 The heaviest damage on Oahu's airbases is suffered at Hickam Field where the first and second Japanese attack waves join forces.

4 At 8:45 A.M., Battleship Row is attacked by a second wave of bombers, while the airfields are raided for a second time.

2 Three minutes after the first attack comes a two-pronged assault, this time from Val divebombers. They home in from the northwest, targeting the aircraft on Hickam Field and the Pearl Harbor Naval Air Force Station.

3 Kates launch their "long lance" torpedoes to the northwest of Ford Island, where carriers are normally berthed, at 7:55 A.M.

"BATTLESHIP ROW"

1 Kate torpedo bombers at high level make up the first wave of the attack on Battleship Row at 7:50 A.M. Further bombs rain down on Pacific bases with initial fatal casualties reported to be 350.

KEY

◄ U.S. SHIPS

✈ JAPANESE AIRCRAFT

MIDWAY *1942*

Dazzling victories—spectacularly at Pearl Harbor—had left Japan keen to strike the U.S. again. One location, favored by fleet commander Admiral Isoruku Yamamoto (1854–1943), was the tiny U.S. mid-Pacific atoll of Midway. His plan was to lure the Americans into a trap by unleashing a diversionary assault on the Aleutians, a string of volcanic islands lying to the north, while the rest of the fleet attacked Midway.

So sure was he of success that Yamamoto committed virtually the entire Japanese fleet to his plan. While it was recognized that Midway represented a gap in Japan's defensive perimeter, there was sharply divided opinion among the Japanese on Yamamoto's proposals, which many believed insufficiently planned.

All reservations, though, were set aside when on April 18, 1942, 16 B-25 Mitchell U.S. bombers took off from aircraft carriers and carried out a surprise attack on

MIDWAY FACTS

Who: Admiral Chester M. Nimitz American Commander in Chief with three carriers, about 70 other warships, and 233 carrier aircraft, together with another 115 planes stationed on Midway itself vs. Rear Admiral Chuichi Nagumo commanding some 160 warships, including eight aircraft carriers, and more than 400 carrier-based aircraft.

What: Aircraft-based battle of the Pacific War resulting in a crushing victory over Japan.

Where: Midway Island, a vulnerable small mid-Pacific atoll, close to Hawaii.

When: June 4–7, 1942.

Why: Owing to faulty intelligence, the Japanese believed the U.S. would be unable

to mount effective opposition to a strike on Midway. By attacking the mid-Atlantic atoll of Midway at the far western end of the Hawaiian chain, Japan hoped to lure the U.S. Pacific Fleet into the open sea and destroy it.

Outcome: Due to Japanese overconfidence and insufficient preparation, the attack was a failure and led to the end of Tokyo's dominance of the Pacific.

LEFT: REAR ADMIRAL FLETCHER'S FLAGSHIP, *the carrier U.S.S.* Yorktown, *is under attack amid heavy flak, while her escort pumps out antiaircraft fire. A series of attacks by Japanese aircraft and a submarine follow.*

Tokyo. Damage was slight, but the attack was a severe blow to Japanese pride. When the case for extending the defense perimeter to Midway and the Aleutians was proposed again, opposition melted. Preparations for a major assault by virtually the entire Japanese navy went ahead at speed.

YAMAMOTO ENCOUNTERS TROUBLE

There was a minor success when, at the start of the attack on Midway, the Japanese succeeded in destroying aircraft on the ground, as well as shooting down 33 planes with only minor losses. But Yamamoto was soon in trouble. His decision to separate his forces into five main groups proved deeply flawed—all were too far apart either to provide support or reinforcement. Additionally, a key role had been given to two Japanese aircraft carriers sent to cover the feint on the Aleutians, but all chances of success were lost when these carriers neglected to join the main force at Midway. As a

RIGHT: MIDWAY BURNS AFTER AN ASSAULT *by enemy forces causes limited damage, leading to the U.S. garrison and its defenses being strengthened.*

BELOW: DAMAGE-CONTROL CREWMEN *make their way across the flight deck of U.S.S. Yorktown, which has to be abandoned after being torpedoed by a submarine on June 7.*

esult, at the time of the battle, the fleet intended to provide he carriers with cover from antiaircraft batteries was 400 iles (650 km) away.

CALCULATED RISK

n anticipation, the attention of all U.S. forces had been on rengthening Midway's garrison, its defense facilities and ortifications. Tactical command of the U.S. force, divided nto two groups, was by Rear Admiral Frank Fletcher 1885–1973), whose resources included the carrier *Yorktown*, hich, through faulty intelligence, the Japanese believed had ready been sunk. Her presence, along with the other arriers, was considered vital by Admiral Chester M. Nimitz 1885–1947), who had total faith in aircraft carriers, with heir ability to strike at long range, in contrast to slower attleships. Fletcher was ordered: "You will be governed by he principle of calculated risk," and told to attack only if here was a fair chance of inflicting disproportionate damage n the Japanese. Carrier planes would attack when it was alculated that Japanese planes would be refueling and their arriers rearmed.

At 4:30 A.M. on June 4, the Carrier Striking Force of dmiral Chuichi Nagumo (1887–1944) launched a strike of 08 aircraft at Midway, spotted immediately on radar. The mericans came out worse in terms of losses, and the airfield

RIGHT: THE FACE OF CONFIDENCE, this aviator, operative within the U.S. Pacific Fleet, is one of a team operating aircraft, notably torpedo bombers, that inflict lethal damage on the Japanese.

was damaged, but it was not knocked out. Nagumo prepared for another attack. At the same time, reports reached him that Japanese ships had come under threat from 10 U.S. warships. A priority had to be established swiftly, particularly as Nagumo's fighters needed refueling. Nagumo cleared his flight decks, rearmed his bombers with torpedoes, and prepared for an all-out attack on the American fleet.

THE MIGHT OF AMERICAN AIR POWER

At 10:20 A.M. he ordered his carriers to turn into the wind and launch their aircraft. Then came the might of American air power: 50 U.S. Dauntless dive bombers catapulted from the skies in pursuit of the Japanese carriers. Nagumo's much vaunted Zero fighters were on the decks or down to sea level after their last dogfight, leaving the skies clear for the U.S. bombers.

On the same morning, 33 Dauntless dive bombers from the carrier Enterprise, under the command of Lieutenant-Commander Wade McClusky (1902–76), had been alerted to hunt for the Japanese First Air Fleet. In Midway's northeast, however, McClusky's aircraft discovered nothing. Unwilling to give up the search, he switched to the west. A while later, he spotted the wake of an enemy destroyer, followed by the sighting of a cluster of Japanese carriers. Flanked by 17 more Dauntlesses from U.S.S. Yorktown, McClusky's fleet unleashed their bombs, screaming down at 325 mph (520km/h). The arrival of Zero fighters was too late to beat off an attack on the aircraft carrier Hiryu. Two other carriers, Kaga and Soryu, were mauled and sunk the same evening, Kaga taking 18 men with it. Hidden by a

LEFT: APPOINTED COMMANDER IN CHIEF of the Japanese Combined Fleet, Isoruku Yamamoto, previously lauded as Japan's premier naval strategist, was ultimately responsible for the disastrous outcome of the Midway assault.

GRUMMAN F4F "WILDCAT" FIGHTER-BOMBER

Although first used in combat by the British in Europe, the Grumman F4F Wildcat, a U.S. carrier-based fighter, was progressed to service with both the U.S. Navy and the Fleet Air Arm, notably in the Pacific theater. Built by General Motors, it remained in service throughout the duration of the war on escort carriers, taking the place of larger and heavier fighters. Wildcats faced a formidable opponent in the Japanese Zero but had a big advantage in superior armor, which enabled badly shot-up aircraft to limp back to base.

RIGHT: AROUND DUSK ON JUNE 6, *the Japanese battlecruiser* Mikuma, *attacked by two air strikes from Midway, sinks, leaving hundreds of her crew to drown.*

squall, *Hiryu* had escaped, advancing ahead of the others as the sole remaining hope of the Japanese. Her response to pursuit had been aggressive, involving the launch of a strike force of 18 divebombers at 11 A.M., with a second force of 10 torpedo planes some two-and-a-half hours later. Aircraft from U.S.S. *Enterprise* and U.S.S. *Yorktown* found their target before 5 P.M., just as *Hiryu* was set to launch its third attack with five bombers and four torpedo aircraft—all she had left.

U.S.S. *Enterprise* aircraft (including 10 refugees from *Yorktown*) attacked *Hiryu* with bombs that put paid to her forward flight deck, setting it on fire. No longer capable of offensive action, she kept moving until around midnight, when flames and an explosion finally stopped her engines. The carrier was abandoned and then torpedoed. Her

captain, together with Rear Admiral Tamon Yamaguchi (1892–1942), Nagumo's deputy, tied themselves to the bridge and went down with the ship. In desperation at his failure, Yamamoto contemplated a surface attack on other U.S. carriers, but could not offer air cover. By then most of the Americans were retreating out of range. Yamamoto recognized defeat, calling off the whole operation and ordering the withdrawal of the fleet.

AFTERMATH

At Midway, the U.S. Pacific Fleet won a remarkable victory. As well as the loss of a carrier, 137 aircraft, and 307 men, the most grievous blow was the loss of U.S.S. *Yorktown*. For the Japanese, defeat meant the loss of its main naval striking force and the end of a dream of destroying the might of U.S. naval power. After winning a clear victory, American forces retired. Japan's loss of four out of their six fleet carriers, plus a large number of their highly trained aircrews, had halted the expansion of the Japanese Empire in the Pacific.

MIDWAY

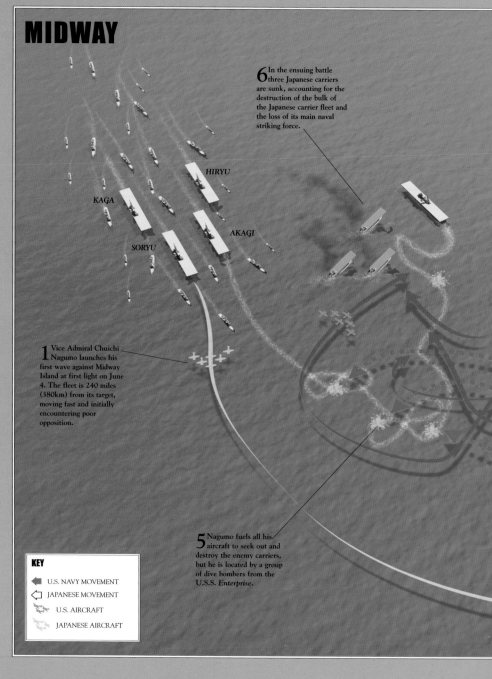

6 In the ensuing battle three Japanese carriers are sunk, accounting for the destruction of the bulk of the Japanese carrier fleet and the loss of its main naval striking force.

HIRYU

KAGA

AKAGI

SORYU

1 Vice Admiral Chuichi Nagumo launches his first wave against Midway Island at first light on June 4. The fleet is 240 miles (380km) from its target, moving fast and initially encountering poor opposition.

5 Nagumo fuels all his aircraft to seek out and destroy the enemy carriers, but he is located by a group of dive bombers from the U.S.S. *Enterprise*.

KEY

◀ U.S. NAVY MOVEMENT

◁ JAPANESE MOVEMENT

U.S. AIRCRAFT

JAPANESE AIRCRAFT

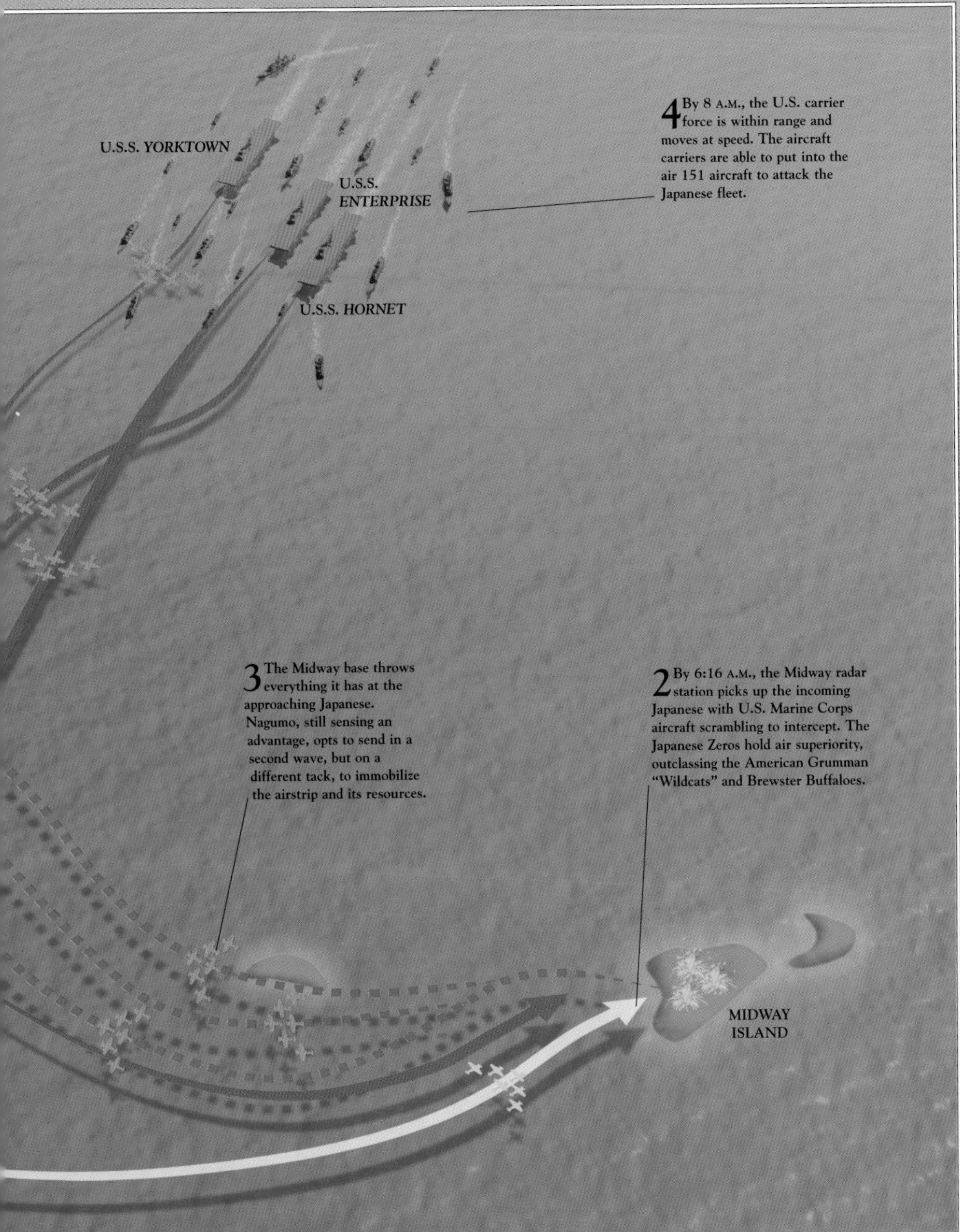

U.S.S. YORKTOWN

U.S.S.
ENTERPRISE

U.S.S. HORNET

4 By 8 A.M., the U.S. carrier force is within range and moves at speed. The aircraft carriers are able to put into the air 151 aircraft to attack the Japanese fleet.

3 The Midway base throws everything it has at the approaching Japanese. Nagumo, still sensing an advantage, opts to send in a second wave, but on a different tack, to immobilize the airstrip and its resources.

2 By 6:16 A.M., the Midway radar station picks up the incoming Japanese with U.S. Marine Corps aircraft scrambling to intercept. The Japanese Zeros hold air superiority, outclassing the American Grumman "Wildcats" and Brewster Buffaloes.

MIDWAY
ISLAND

STALINGRAD 1943

After a bitter siege, the Sixth Army of General Friedrich Paulus (1890–1957) of the German Wehrmacht surrendered to the Soviet Red Army at Stalingrad on January 31, 1943. At its height, the Germans had captured 90 percent of the city. But it was an achievement Adolf Hitler (1889–1945) threw away, following blunders and miscalculations.

With the launch of Operation *Barbarossa* (Nazi Germany's invasion of the Soviet Union) massive artillery and armor were unleashed over the German-Russian front, stretching from the Baltic to the Black Sea. The Crimea had been reached in the south, along with Leningrad in the north and the prospect of seizing Moscow was at hand.

Dazzled by these early successes, Hitler was determined to seize the oil-rich Caucasus. Deaf to all advice, he went on to split his forces in two, one to push across the Don River toward Stalingrad, the other to head southward. His generals

STALINGRAD FACTS

Who: German General Friedrich Paulus, Commander of Sixth Army; Georgi Zhukov, Marshal and Deputy Supreme Commander, organizing the relief of Stalingrad; Vasily Chuikov, Commander of Sixty-Second Army in Stalingrad.

What: Stalingrad was the greatest single defeat of German arms since the Napoleonic wars. More than 130,000 men went into Soviet captivity. Axis casualties were estimated to be 750,000 killed, wounded, or captured.

Where: Stalingrad, today Volgograd, Hitler's prime objective, an extended industrial city of 500,000 inhabitants stretching along 18 miles (29km) of the west bank of the Volga River.

When: August 23, 1942–January 31, 1943.

Why: Stalingrad afforded a vital transportation route between the Caspian Sea and northern Russia. Its capture would have secured the left flank of the German armies as they advanced into the oil-rich Caspian Sea and Caucasus region.

Outcome: With its defeat at Stalingrad, all claims to combat invincibility were destroyed irrevocably for the German army.

LEFT: *GERMAN TROOPS ASSAULT THE SUBURBS OF STALINGRAD, which is heavily bomb-damaged. Opposition is a lot tougher than expected. A hard winter lies ahead.*

protested, hazarding a guess that Stalin could summon 1,500,000 men north of Stalingrad with 50,000 in the Caucasus. On the eastern front, the Axis had 232 divisions; 61 were from the allies of Romania, Italy, Finland, and Hungary and all of them were poorly equipped.

At dawn on Sunday, August 23, 1942, the tanks of Germany's 16th Panzer Division crossed the Don River, supported by some 600 Junkers and Stukas aircraft. Stemming the buildup of Soviet forces was entrusted to Field Marshal Wilhelm List of Army Group B, to the north of the city. Hitler was so confident that Stalingrad (with a population of 500,000) would soon fall that he transferred one of his key groups, Fourth Panzer Army to help out the south in the push to reach the Caucusus and the oil-rich area around the Caspian Sea. That left the Sixth Army under General Friedrich Paulus (1890–1957) to take Stalingrad alone. Colonel-General Franz Halder (1884–1972), Hitler's Chief of Staff, argued that Sixth Army would weaken seriously without the support of the Fourth Panzer Army. Hitler, who by this time had taken over the day-to-day running of the war, brusquely dismissed all protests.

NOT A STEP BACKWARD!

Stalingrad, with its network of grim concrete industrial sites becoming fortresses, had long been preparing for war. Stalin (1879–1953) ordered all troops "Ni shagu nazad!" ("Not a step backward!"), reinforced with the slogan, "There is no land beyond the Volga." General Georgi Constantinovich Zhukov (1896–1974), hero of the previous winter's defense of Moscow, was now Deputy Supreme Commander, and General Vasili

BELOW: THIS EPIC PAINTING from the post-war era shows Red Army troops preparing to cross the Volga to fight in the city of Stalingrad.

Chuikov (1900–82) of Sixty-Second Army controlled the city's defenses.

The Germans began their assault on the outer part of the city in August. By late September, the Sixth Army had become bogged down in close urban warfare in the suburbs of the city. Hitler's generals became increasingly worried at the wide dispersal of vulnerable forces. Romanian armies manned the left flank of the German Army Group B, the closest to Stalingrad, with Italian and Hungarian divisions farther to the west. Hitler ignored all doubters, proclaiming: "Where the German soldier sets foot, there he remains."

General Paulus's orders were to battle through Stalingrad to the Volga River. The German heavyweight assault was Paulus's infantry and General Hermann Hoth's (1885–1971) panzers, driving in from the west and south. The main ferry landing was safely secured, but Paulus knew that, with the weather, the Volga would freeze, enabling the enemy to send increasing reinforcements over the ice.

Within Stalingrad, Chuikov had overseen the training of heavily armed snipers, who operated on a house-to-house basis, picking off those Germans who had reached the city and were stumbling from one building to another. On October 4, Paulus's Sixth Army launched an assault on Tractor Factory, the "Barricades" arms plants and the Red October steelworks. These three heavily fortified areas formed the hard nucleus of the Sixty-Second Army's defense of the city. After much hard fighting, where buildings often changed hands a number of times in the same day, the entire area had been reduced to a tiny enclave.

SOVIET COUNTEROFFENSIVE

However, outside of Stalingrad, the Soviets were preparing a masterful counteroffensive to trap the Sixth Army. By the

*ABOVE: A GERMAN PLATOON PREPARES TO ATTACK the factory district.
To the right is a column of Sturmgeschütz III (Stug III) assault guns, highly
effective tank destroyers often used for assaulting fixed positions.*

middle of November, using the landings across the Volga,
Zhukov had summoned more than a million men, some
13,500 heavy guns, 900 tanks, and 1,100 aircraft. Frantically,
Paulus begged for more supplies, but these proved sparse.
Called Operation *Uranus*, the Red Army's counteroffensive
sought the utter destruction of Hitler's forces in the southern
Soviet Union, with two fresh armies striking southeastward
toward the Don River, northwest of Stalingrad. Then, from
the south, two more armies would strike northwest. Squeezed
in a pincer would be Germany's Sixth Army and a part of
Fourth Panzer Army.

On the bitterly cold night of November 18/19, the
Romanian forces to the northwest of Stalingrad faced a
massive artillery barrage followed by an armored assault. They
lacked the necessary fuel and were powerless to counter

*RIGHT: EXPERT SOVIET SNIPERS TARGET vulnerable Wehrmacht troops who
struggle through an unfamiliar network of buildings.*

ABOVE: FOR THE BENEFIT OF CAMERAS, *a Russian flag is waved to signify triumphant victory over the burning hell of Stalingrad. Soviet losses were to exceed 750,000 servicemen and civilians.*

T-34/76 MODEL 1943

The Soviet T-34/76 tank, of which this was a 1943 model, is one of the main variants of the T-34 medium tank. It was so highly regarded that it remained the mainstay of the armed forces well into the Cold War. Its major advantages are speedy assembly and heavy armor protection, as well as excellent cross-country performance in difficult terrain and snowy conditions.

Soviet firepower. Survivors were overwhelmed within hours. A gaping 50-mile (80-km) hole was left in the Axis lines to the northwest of the city. Trapped inside the arms of the Soviet Russian pincer were 200,000 German, Italian, and Romanian soldiers.

HITLER REFUSES TO LEAVE THE VOLGA

Chief of Staff Colonel-General Franz Halder (1884–1972), forever pressing the increasingly obdurate Hitler to allow Paulus's Sixth Army to fight its way free, was dismissed, replaced by General Kurt Zeitler (1895–1963), who took the same line as Halder. Paulus pleaded, "It is essential to withdraw all our divisions from Stalingrad." Hitler riposted: "I won't leave the Volga! I won't go back from the Volga!" On November 25, 1942, Hitler summoned Field Marshal Erich von Manstein (1887–1973) to head the newly created Army Group Don, pushing from the southwest to relieve Sixth Army. Manstein informed

ABOVE: THIS KNOCKED-OUT SOVIET T-70 LIGHT TANK, in action during Operation Uranus, is one of a number that proved too vulnerable to penetrate the superior armor of its German opponents.

ABOVE: A RED ARMY SOLDIER armed with a PPSh-41 sub-machinegun looks out from behind a tree. By the winter of 1942 the Soviets were able to issue winter camouflage suits to most of their frontline troops.

Hitler that the enemy was too strong, only to be told to fight his way to Sixth Army, which must remain in Stalingrad.

LUFTWAFFE IS HELPLESS TO ASSIST

Hitler next turned to *Luftwaffe* chief Hermann Goering (1893–1946), who boasted that his *Luftwaffe* could save Sixth Army by feeding and arming it by air and safely evacuating the wounded.

But Sixth Army's daily needs included 120 tons of fuel and 250 tons of ammunition, which would have required 165 flights each day, taking no account of future food needs. Fog hindered many flights and, at best, only 140 tons got through. Despite this setback, Hitler forbade a breakout. The Soviets counterattacked on the Upper Don River, sweeping aside the Italian Eighth Army and wheeling south to threaten Manstein's rear. Hoth's Fourth Panzer Army was ordered to withdraw from the west of Stalingrad to avoid complete destruction.

"CAPITULATION IS IMPOSSIBLE!"

Inside the beleaguered city during Christmas 1942 frostbite, dysentery, and typhus raged. On December 26, Paulus radioed that he could only hold out for days. On January 8 1943, the Germans were given the chance by the Soviets to surrender. Paulus signaled Hitler, asking for freedom of action. Hitler replied: "Capitulation is impossible. The Sixth Army will do its historic duty at Stalingrad until the last man." On January 30, Paulus radioed Hitler: "Final collapse cannot be delayed more than 24 hours."

In a bid to stiffen his resolve, Hitler promoted Paulus to Field Marshal. But Paulus ignored Hitler's orders and surrendered the Sixth Army. The Battle of Stalingrad was finally over.

AFTERMATH

With the signing of the surrender, virtually the entire city lay in ruins. Along the Stalingrad front, 300,000 Germans were killed or captured, along with 450,000 allies. Russian losses totaled 750,000, including many civilians.

STALINGRAD

RYNOK

FACTORY
DISTRICT

5 Throughout October, the Germans hold their advantage in the factory district, enabling them to command control of 90 percent of the city. This advantage ultimately proves short-lived.

3 On September 27, the Germans attack the fiercely defended northern factory district in an attempt to block the landing stages lying nearby.

KEY

◄ GERMAN MOVEMENT

⊠ GERMAN INFANTRY DIVISION

▱ GERMAN PANZER DIVISION

▱ GERMAN MOTORIZED DIVISION

4 At a price high in military and civilian casualties, the Soviets hold onto their supply lines across the Volga, enabling Sixty-Second Army to maintain its foothold in the city.

LANDING STAGE

KRASNAYA SLOBODA

MAMAYEV KURGAN

GRAIN SILO

RIVER VOLGA

1 German LI Corps make a bid to capture the high hill landmark of Mamayev Kurgan and the central landing stage for Red Army forces by the Volga.

2 Engaged in support of German forces to the south, the Fourth Panzer Army encounters severe resistance from forces within the grain silo dominating the city.

DIEN BIEN PHU

1954

After World War II, the government of France sought to reassert dominion over a far-flung colonial empire, which had been destabilized during years of fighting and the occupation of France by Nazi Germany. In Southeast Asia, the French reestablished their colonial government in Indochina, which had been occupied by the Japanese.

From the beginning, however, nationalism posed a threat to the stability of the entire region. As early as 1946, the Viet Minh, insurgents inspired by the blended philosophy of communism and nationalism espoused by their leader, Ho Chi Minh (1890–1969), were conducting a guerrilla war against the French, hoping to create the independent nation of Vietnam. By the fall of 1953, a succession of French military commanders had failed to subdue the Viet Minh and pacify the

DIEN BIEN PHU FACTS

Who: Colonel Christian de Castries and 16,000 French, colonial, and loyal Vietnamese soldiers versus General Vo Nguyen Giap (born 1911) and 50,000 Viet Minh troops.

What: The communist Viet Minh and French forces fought the decisive battle of the French campaign to retain their colony of Indochina.

Where: The valley and surrounding mountains of Dien Bien Phu in northwestern Vietnam.

When: March 13–May 7, 1954.

Why: The French sought to destroy the Viet Minh in a set-piece battle.

Outcome: Dien Bien Phu was a decisive victory for the Viet Minh, who utilized superior artillery and overwhelming numbers during a successful siege.

LEFT: *Following their capitulation at Dien Bien Phu, French prisoners are marched into captivity, closely watched by attentive Viet Minh guards.*

ABOVE: *ALREADY ON THE GROUND, a pair of French paratroopers watch more airborne troops descend into the area around the base at Dien Bien Phu.*
RIGHT: *VIET MINH COMMANDER VO NGUYEN GIAP discusses strategy with subordinate commanders during planning for operations at Dien Bien Phu.*

country. Utilizing hit-and-run tactics, the guerrillas had confounded French army efforts to force them into a decisive battle.

Therefore, General Henri Navarre (1898–1983), who had been appointed to overall command of French forces the previous spring, authorized the establishment of a base of operations in the extreme northwest at Dien Bien Phu, in Lai Chau province, near the frontiers with Laos and China. At long last, Navarre believed, the Viet Minh could be drawn into a set-piece engagement and defeated by superior French firepower.

WHY DIEN BIEN PHU?

For months, the French armed forces in Indochina had suffered from a lack of clear objectives and conducted reactionary operations while the Viet Minh seized the initiative and had taken control of part of Laos to facilitate the movement of troops and supplies. As Navarre contemplated the most effective means of countering the Viet Minh successes and restoring the morale of his own forces, a member of his staff suggested the implementation of a "hedgehog" principle. The plan was to fortify a base in the northwest, behind areas of strong Viet Minh activity, and compel the communists to protect their supply lines in a decisive battle.

As plans for the air-land operation progressed, the abandoned airstrip at Dien Bien Phu, constructed by the Japanese during World War II, was chosen for the French initiation of Operation *Castor*. The selection of Dien Bien Phu has been criticized for several reasons, chiefly the distance from supply sources, the fact that resupply had to take place by air, and the lay of the land. The French positions at Dien Bien Phu were located in a river valley stretching about 10 miles (16km) and surrounded by high ground. General Vo Nguyen Giap (1911–), commander of the Viet Minh forces, described the area as a rice bowl, the French at the bottom and his Viet Minh around the rim.

RECIPE FOR DISASTER

When the initial contingent of 9,000 French airborne troops parachuted or were flown into Dien Bien Phu on November 20, 1953, they did not attempt to seize the high ground around their base. The French position was to be defended by a series of nine strongpoints in the valley and lower hills. These were designated Gabrielle, Beatrice, and Anne-Marie to the north, Huguette, Francoise, and Claudine to the west, Dominique and Eliane to the east, and Isabelle in the south. Some detractors asserted that the names were those of various mistresses of the French ground commander, Colonel Christian de Castries (1902–91). The more likely source of their origin is the first nine letters of the alphabet.

Perhaps the most glaring error in the French plan was their underestimation of Viet Minh resolve. Giap ordered communist units in the vicinity to resist as best they could while he marshaled strong forces. As the buildup of French troops at Dien Bien Phu swelled to about 16,000 airborne, Foreign Legion, Colonial, and loyal Vietnamese during the spring of 1954, the Viet Minh massed five divisions in the rugged mountains. At peak strength, the Viet Minh forces totaled about 50,000. Giap knew that time and terrain were on his side.

In a remarkable feat of logistics, guerrillas and civilian laborers manhandled 200 artillery pieces up steep mountain trails and dug camouflaged emplacements that were virtually undetectable from the valley floor. One Viet Minh veteran of Dien Bien Phu remembered a comrade flinging himself under the wheels of an artillery piece that had broken free of its lines in order to prevent

FRENCH PARATROOPER

The airborne forces were an elite component of the French Army, which was defeated at Dien Bien Phu. In full battle dress, this paratrooper carries supplies and ammunition for his automatic weapon, which is slung over his shoulder. Although they fought bravely at Dien Bien Phu, the French underestimated the capabilities of their Viet Minh adversaries.

the weapon rolling into a ravine. Large numbers of antiaircraft guns were brought in to counter French airpower and interdict reinforcement and resupply efforts. By the time the first Viet Minh artillery shells came crashing down on Dien Bien Phu in January 1954, the communists outgunned the French four to one and had encircled the lodgment.

ABOVE: VIET MINH SOLDIERS PAUSE *between attacks against French trenches at Dien Bien Phu. Heavy Viet Minh artillery was a deciding factor in the outcome of the siege.*

THE BATTLE JOINED

After more than three months of preparations, Giap ordered the capture of Beatrice on March 13. The onslaught began with direct artillery fire. A single shell hit the command post, killing the commander of the 13th Foreign Legion Demi-Brigade defending the position along with his entire staff. At a cost of 600 dead and 1,200 wounded, Beatrice fell to the Viet Minh in no

more than seven hours. Distraught over his inability to direct effective counter-battery fire against the heavy Viet Minh guns, the French artillery commander, Colonel Charles Piroth (1906–1954) committed suicide with a hand grenade.

When the communist reduction of the French positions began in earnest, the guerrillas had excavated more than 62 miles (100 km) of trenches around the northern redoubts. After the capture of Beatrice, they tightened the noose further, taking Gabrielle during two days of attack and counterattack.

The airfield was shut down by concentrated antiaircraft fire, which made it impossible for planes to land. Resupply was sporadic and only by parachute from an altitude that rendered most drops inaccurate. More badly needed provisions plummeted to the Viet Minh than to the French. On March 17, Anne-Marie was abandoned to the communists.

For two more weeks, the Viet Minh continued to dig trenches and harass the tiring French, who were enduring a brutal existence, tending hundreds of wounded with dwindling medical supplies under continuous artillery fire. By March 30, the 1,000 defenders of Isabelle were cut off. At the end of April, the battered French clung only to portions of Huguette, Dominique, and Eliane. On May 7, vigorous Viet Minh attacks threatened to overrun the remaining French strongpoints, and de Castries realized that further resistance was futile. When he spoke with his commanding officer, General René Cogny (1904–68), in the provincial capital at Hanoi 220 miles (355 km) away, his primary concern was for the care of the wounded. On the subject of surrender, Cogny was emphatic: "…Of course, you have to finish the whole thing now. But what you have done until now surely is magnificent. Don't spoil it by hoisting the white flag…no surrender, no white flag."

EPILOGUE

The fall of Dien Bien Phu on May 8, 1954, was a humiliation for France and effectively ended the nation's involvement in Vietnam. The communists had captured nearly 12,000 prisoners, including 5,000 wounded, and about 1,150 French soldiers had died. Viet Minh casualties were 8,000

ABOVE: *CELEBRATING THEIR GREAT VICTORY over the French at Dien Bien Phu, Viet Minh soldiers accept the accolades of the public.*

LEFT: *FRENCH SOLDIERS REST during a lull in the fighting at Dien Bien Phu. They have just led a counterattack against Viet Minh forces attempting to capture their position.*

dead and more than 15,000 wounded. Giap had paid a high price, but he had achieved a tremendous victory.

Later in 1954, the Geneva Accords divided Vietnam at the 17th parallel. The communist north was supported by the Soviet Union and the People's Republic of China, while the south, which did not ascribe to the terms at Geneva, was backed by the United States. Further conflict was inevitable. The last French soldiers left Vietnam in 1956 as the colonial empire they had bravely defended continued to crumble.

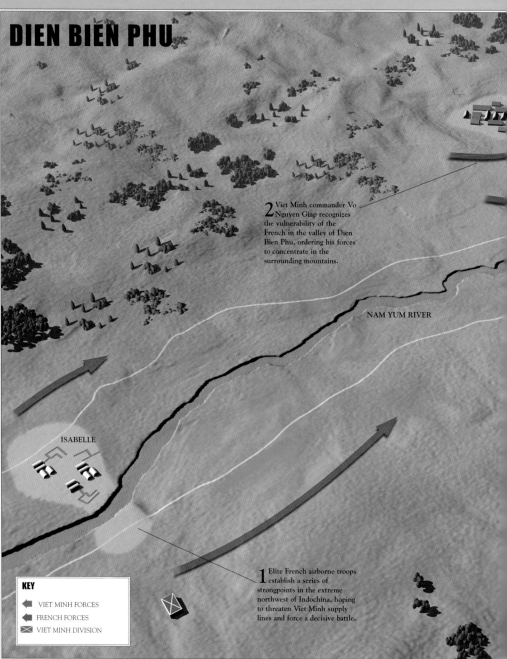

DIEN BIEN PHU

2 Viet Minh commander Vo Nguyen Giap recognizes the vulnerability of the French in the valley of Dien Bien Phu, ordering his forces to concentrate in the surrounding mountains.

NAM YUM RIVER

ISABELLE

1 Elite French airborne troops establish a series of strongpoints in the extreme northwest of Indochina, hoping to threaten Viet Minh supply lines and force a decisive battle.

KEY

◀ VIET MINH FORCES

◀ FRENCH FORCES

✉ VIET MINH DIVISION

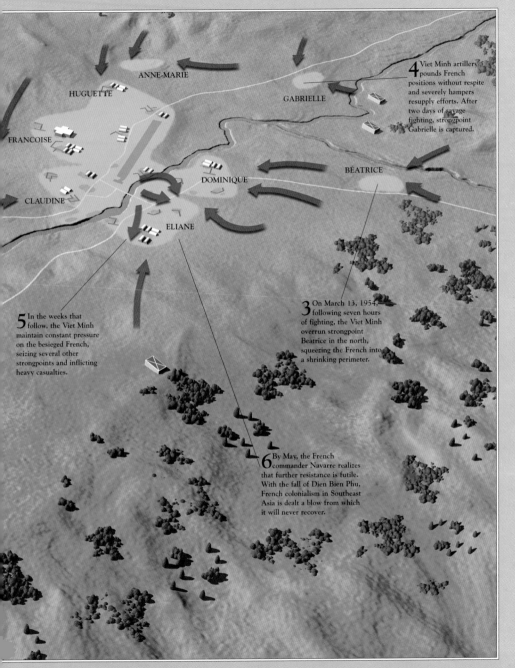

ANNE-MARIE

HUGUETTE

GABRIELLE

FRANCOISE

4 Viet Minh artillery pounds French positions without respite and severely hampers resupply efforts. After two days of savage fighting, strongpoint Gabrielle is captured.

DOMINIQUE

BÉATRICE

CLAUDINE

ELIANE

5 In the weeks that follow, the Viet Minh maintain constant pressure on the besieged French, seizing several other strongpoints and inflicting heavy casualties.

3 On March 13, 1954, following seven hours of fighting, the Viet Minh overrun strongpoint Beatrice in the north, squeezing the French into a shrinking perimeter.

6 By May, the French commander Navarre realizes that further resistance is futile. With the fall of Dien Bien Phu, French colonialism in Southeast Asia is dealt a blow from which it will never recover.

LONGEWALA 1971

Border forces serve mainly in a security and "tripwire" role, imposing a little delay and warning the main body that an enemy is on the move. While it is expected that small forces will try to hold their position as long as possible, the stand made by "A" Company of the 23rd Battalion of the Punjab Regiment turned out to be one of the decisive actions of the war.

The British retreat from South Asia left behind two new nations on the Indian Ocean coast. India occupied the subcontinent, while Pakistan was divided into two areas by Indian territory. West Pakistan was relatively rich and home to most of the nation's industry as well as the ruling class. East Pakistan (modern Bangladesh) served as a breadbasket, but the people there received little benefit from their membership of the new country, and discontent gradually increased.

The political situation in Pakistan was troubled and rife with internal disputes. Elections held in 1970 precipitated a crisis when Sheik Rahman (1920–75), an East

LONGEWALA FACTS

Who: A small Indian force under Major Kuldip Singh Chandpuri, opposed by a much larger Pakistani formation under Brigadier Tariq Mir.

What: Indian defenders fought a hard delaying action until air support and reinforcements turned the battle.

Where: Border post at Longewala on the India–Pakistan border.

When: December 5, 1971.

Why: Pakistani forces sought to enter India and capture the strategically important town of Jaisalmer, necessitating passage at Longewala.

Outcome: A decisive Indian victory. Major Kuldip Singh Chandpuri was decorated with India's second highest gallantry award, the Maha Vir Chakra. Other members of the defending company were also decorated.

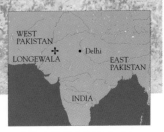

LEFT: *Though not a cutting-edge weapon system in 1971, the U.S-built M47 tanks of the Pakistani army were entirely capable of overrunning a lightly manned border post.*

Pakistani leader, emerged with a majority. This threatened vested interests in the west of the country and General Yahya Khan (1917–80), decided to use the army to alter the political landscape. The Sheik was arrested and martial law imposed in East Pakistan.

General Yahya tried to intimidate the people of East Pakistan using the army, which was largely of West Pakistani origins. This resulted in a major insurrection and a flood of refugees pouring into India, where they strained local resources. The Pakistani army's habit of chasing insurgents into India caused a series of clashes with Indian forces. Relations between India and Pakistan were not good, and after trying to get assistance via the United Nations, India decided to go to war with Pakistan. The buildup of forces was obvious, and the Pakistani military had plenty of time to react.

The Indian strategy was to hold the Pakistanis in the west while undertaking offensive operations in the east to clear that flank. Interior lines of communication would then allow forces to be transferred to the western theater where the bulk and best of the Pakistani army would take longer to deal with. Pakistan meanwhile knew that victory was impossible in the

BELOW: A PAKISTANI TANK struggles to gain traction in the desert along the India-Pakistan border. At Longewala, many Pakistani AFVs became stuck in the soft sand, making them easy targets for the Indian Air Force Hunters.

INDIAN PARATROOPER

British influences are obvious in the arms and equipment of this Indian Army paratrooper. He is armed with a FN-FAL semiautomatic 0.3-inch (7.62 mm) rifle, the same weapon used by the British army of the time. Paratroops are more often used as elite infantry than in their ostensible airborne-assault role. Paratroop formations are necessarily "light" formations, with little heavy equipment and transport. They are thus often assigned artillery and other support from the nonair-mobile component of the army when functioning in the infantry role. Without such support, the paras are highly effective for a short time but rapidly decline in combat efficiency as their limited supplies are used up.

188

east and resolved to tie up Indian strength there for as long as possible while trying for a victory in the west. The first move was a preemptive air strike on December 3, 1971, intended to cripple Indian air power on the ground as the Israelis had done to Egypt in 1967. The air strike was not a success, and the Indian air force was able to give extensive support to the ground troops throughout the short war that followed.

ADVANCE ON LONGEWALA

At Longewala, 120 men of "A" Company, 23rd Battalion, Punjab regiment, held the border post. They had some mortars and two recoilless rifles mounted on jeeps for support. Against this tiny force the Pakistani army sent an entire infantry brigade backed up by more than 60 tanks and an artillery detachment.

The post was on the alert and a patrol detected the Pakistani force approaching. The commander, Major

BELOW: THIS PAKISTANI TANK HAS BECOME A TROPHY OF WAR for the Indian Army. Pakistani armored forces came close to overrunning the outpost at Longewala. They were halted by a combination of reserve forces, air attack, and a very stubborn defense by the unit in place when the attack began.

Chandpuri, immediately asked for support from battalion headquarters some 10 miles (17 km) away. Artillery shells were already landing in the Indian positions, killing five camels but doing little other damage.

The Pakistani force came into sight at about 4 A.M. on December 5. Battalion headquarters gave Major Chandpuri the option to retreat or make a stand on his own initiative. He announced that he would hold his position to the death. His inspiring leadership was a critical factor in the battle that followed.

THE FIRST ATTACK

There had been no time to lay the mines that had been issued to the Indian troops, so antitank defense rested with two recoilless rifles mounted on jeeps. These opened fire and disabled an enemy tank, a Chinese-built T-59, almost immediately. A jeep carrying a senior Pakistani officer was also hit. This brought the attack to a halt in some confusion and several more tanks were disabled. Three more lost their tracks to mines thrown in their path by an audacious Indian soldier before he was killed. Meanwhile, Indian machine-guns

and mortars caused considerable casualties among the infantry. However, some tanks were creeping around the sand dunes, looking for a way to attack from the flank or rear, and the situation was becoming desperate.

AIR SUPPORT ARRIVES

At dawn, Hawker Hunters from the nearest Indian airbase were able to take off and found themselves in a target-rich environment. Rockets destroyed several tanks and when those ran out, the Hunters tried out their 1.2-in (30-mm) cannon in the tank-busting role. This worked quite well too, with several tanks set afire.

The air strike caused a panic among the Pakistani tanks, many driving frantically around in circles to throw off enemy pilots' aim. During the confusion, two companies of Indian infantry and some light tanks with artillery support arrived to reinforce Longewala. The patrol that had initially detected the enemy also came in to join the defense.

THE FINAL ATTACKS

Between 11 A.M. and 12 noon the Pakistanis made two more attempts to break the Longewala position. The first was somewhat disorganized and took heavy casualties before being beaten off. The second was a more considered set-piece attack by a battalion of infantry supported by tanks and artillery.

A greatly reinforced defense, backed up by air strikes, met the final attack and soon it was bogged down. After a while the Pakistani forces suddenly pulled back and broke contact, leaving 37 tanks destroyed along with a train that had been bringing reinforcements in when it was spotted by Air Force pilots and savaged with rockets.

Major Chandpuri had sworn to defend his post to the death, but in the event three Indian soldiers were killed, and three more were injured.

OUTCOMES

Pakistani losses were considerable. In addition to the tanks destroyed outright, many more were abandoned due to damage, mechanical failures, or becoming bogged down in the soft sand. Almost 100 other vehicles were also destroyed or lost, and 200 soldiers were killed. However, it was the operational and psychological results that were most important. A breakthrough at Longewala would have allowed Pakistani

BELOW: INDIAN FORCES WERE ABLE TO ADVANCE into Pakistan before the war ended, placing India in a strong position for the ceasefire negotiations. Had Longewala not held out, the reverse might have been true.

ABOVE: *LIEUTENANT-GENERAL NIAZI SURRENDERS Pakistani forces in East Pakistan to Lieutenant-General Aurora, December 16, 1971.*

LEFT: *INDIAN INFANTRY PASS A DESTROYED Pakistani tank during the Indian-Pakistan War.*

forces to strike deep into India, perhaps capturing territory that would have been useful at the negotiating table. However, the entire operation was derailed by failure at Longewala, and morale on both sides was also greatly affected.

The Indo-Pakistani war ended on December 16, 1971, with India victorious. East Pakistan was lost; the only way to retain it would have been to capture Indian territory and trade one for the other at the peace conference. However, Pakistan ended the war with little to trade. Thus East Pakistan became the independent nation of Bangladesh.

REASONS WHY

The advance on Longewala may have been ill considered, in that the Pakistani tanks were known to find sandy terrain difficult. Air cover would have been invaluable but was not provided, to great cost. However, given the overwhelming force in use, it was reasonable to assume that the post would be either abandoned or quickly overrun. Without the courage and determination of a badly outmatched Indian force, the operation would probably have gone off without undue difficulty before the Indian Air Force was able to intervene. However, once the attack had been initially stalled, the weaknesses in the plan became clear and resulted in a massive defeat and heavy casualties.

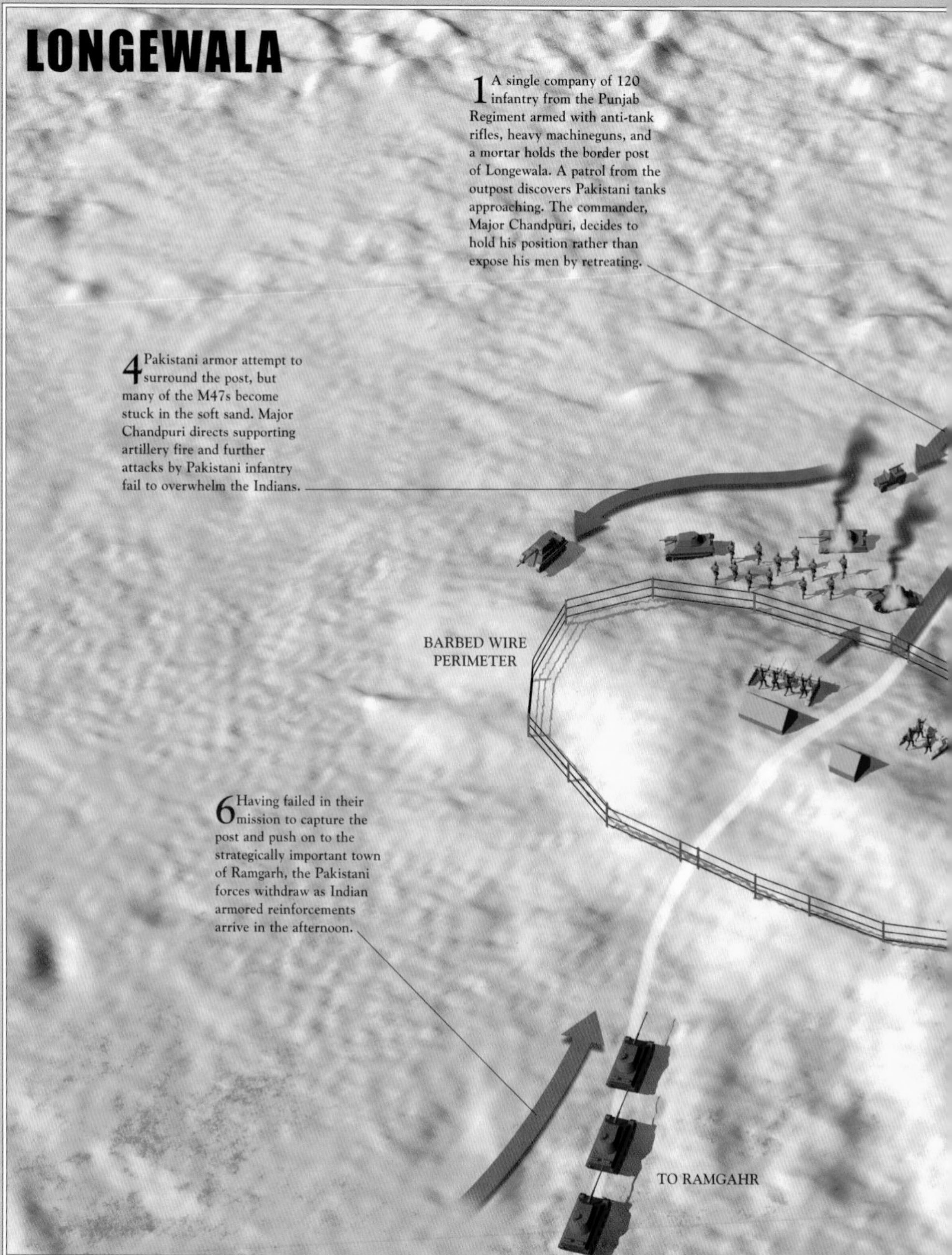

LONGEWALA

1 A single company of 120 infantry from the Punjab Regiment armed with anti-tank rifles, heavy machineguns, and a mortar holds the border post of Longewala. A patrol from the outpost discovers Pakistani tanks approaching. The commander, Major Chandpuri, decides to hold his position rather than expose his men by retreating.

4 Pakistani armor attempt to surround the post, but many of the M47s become stuck in the soft sand. Major Chandpuri directs supporting artillery fire and further attacks by Pakistani infantry fail to overwhelm the Indians.

BARBED WIRE
PERIMETER

6 Having failed in their mission to capture the post and push on to the strategically important town of Ramgarh, the Pakistani forces withdraw as Indian armored reinforcements arrive in the afternoon.

TO RAMGAHR

2 A brigade of Pakistani infantry and 65 M47 tanks begins to attack along the road at 12.30 a.m. The defenders hastily lay anti-tank mines along the approach. Firing from high sand dunes, the Indians knock out a number of M47 tanks from close range with their anti-tank rifles.

3 The Pakistani attack stalls for two hours as they wait for sappers to clear the minefield. The scene becomes more confused as the smoke from the burning tanks covers the area.

5 Dawn arrives and Hawker Hunter ground attack aircraft from the Indian Air Force come to the aid of the defenders. By midday, a further 22 Pakistani tanks have been destroyed by air attack, many of the M47s easy targets in the soft sand.

INDIAN AIR
SUPPORT

KEY

◄ INDIAN MOVEMENT

◄ PAKISTANI MOVEMENT

MOGADISHU 1993

Urban combat has always been a difficult and dangerous proposition. In the cluttered terrain of a city, ill-armed and untrained insurgents can inflict heavy casualties on regular forces. The Battle of Mogadishu was a success in some ways for U.S. forces but the cost was considered too high to be acceptable.

Somalia in the early 1990s was a very troubled place. A coup toppled President Mohammed Siad Barre (1919–95) in January 1991, and soon afterward the coalition that had launched the coup fragmented. Thus began a period of bitter infighting for the leadership of the nation.

The conflict wrecked Somalia's agricultural base and resulted in starvation for thousands of people. Humanitarian aid was provided, but gangs loyal to the various factions stole most of it and either used it to supply military operations or else sold it to buy weapons. The answer was to provide military protection for the aid convoys and the personnel who operated them. Troops from the U.S. and

MOGADISHU FACTS

Who: Fewer than 200 U.S. Army and Special Forces troops, supported by helicopters and Malaysian and Pakistani ground forces, opposed by a total of up to 2,000–3,000 irregular Somalian insurgents.

What: U.S. Rangers became pinned down near a crashed helicopter.

Where: Mogadishu, capital of Somalia.

When: October 3–4, 1993.

Why: U.S. forces entered the city to capture senior personnel loyal to Mohamed Farrah Aidid, a terrorist warlord.

Outcome: The trapped unit was rescued but suffered unacceptable casualties, with United States forces suffering 18 killed and 79 men wounded during the operation.

YEMEN

ETHIOPIA

SOMALIA
✚ Mogadishu

LEFT: A U.S. MARINE ON PATROL IN MOGADISHU IN 1993. *Military forces were required to operate in cramped urban environments yet were restricted by strict rules of engagement.*

BLACKHAWK HELICOPTER

The Sikorsky UH-60 Blackhawk is the U.S. Army's standard tactical transport helicopter. It can also serve in other roles, including medical evacuation, transport of senior personnel, electronic warfare, and border enforcement. An Army Blackhawk can carry 11 troops as a tactical transport, allowing rapid movement in the field. In the last 20 years, Blackhawks have served in this capacity in Panama, Grenada, The Balkans, Iraq, and Afghanistan.

There was nothing different about the Blackhawks' mission in Somalia, other than the fact that it was carried out in dense urban terrain. This exposed the helicopters to the risk of ground fire from concealed positions, or from locations where suppressive return fire was not possible due to the proximity of noncombatants. Experience in Mogadishu, and later in Iraq, showed that helicopters are vulnerable in urban terrain and forced a change in U.S. military doctrine.

RIGHT: A SOMALIAN MILITIAMAN SITS with his RPG-7 launcher resting on his lap. The RPG has proved a deadly and effective weapon in many theaters of war, partly because it can be easily handled by relatively unskilled operators.

other nations, notably Pakistan and Malaysia, were deployed for the purpose. In addition, efforts were made to seek a peaceful solution to the conflict and ultimately to restore order in the country. Most factions agreed to the terms of the deal, though the faction answering to General Mohammed Farrah Aidid (1934–96), former chairman of the Somali National Alliance, remained recalcitrant. Aidid's faction was either responsible for, or at least permitted other insurgents to carry out, an attack that killed 24 Pakistani peacekeepers in Mogadishu.

It was decided to launch an operation to capture Aidid's senior staff using a combination of helicopter assault and a ground force moving fast through the streets. Named Operation *Irene*, the plan was to strike rapidly to secure the targets using special forces troops rappelling from helicopters, while a support force moved through the streets to pick up and remove the detainees.

OPERATION IRENE BEGINS

As the ground and air components began their transit across the city, unexpectedly fierce resistance began to appear. Barricades thrown up by insurgents slowed the ground team, and vehicles were attacked with RPG-7

launchers. The air component was also attacked with the same weapons. Unguided grenade launchers are not ideal weapons with which to engage aircraft, but a slow-moving helicopter presents a target not much different from a ground vehicle. And the RPG-7 warhead is large enough to do serious damage if it hits.

A LONG NIGHT IN MOGADISHU

One of the Blackhawk helicopters of the assault force was shot down by an RPG-7, and the rescue helicopter sent to assist it was also hit. Despite this, using kevlar plates from the downed Blackhawk to create a bulletproof shelter, the rescue team was able to move the five wounded survivors to a suitable point for pickup. A force of about 90 army Rangers was detached to rescue the helicopter crews, and became surrounded near the crash site. With extraction impossible and night soon to fall, the Rangers took up positions in nearby houses and prepared to fight for their lives.

Meanwhile a second Blackhawk was shot down. Two Delta Force operatives insisted on being taken in by

helicopter to protect the pilot. Both were eventually killed and the pilot taken prisoner.

The Rangers near the first crash site found themselves surrounded and under attack from all sides. They had captured several civilians when they occupied the houses, and chose to retain the captives. This was perhaps just as well, because the insurgent commander had decided to mortar the Rangers' position into wreckage rather than make an assault, and the presence of the civilians made this an unattractive option. However, it did not prevent Somali gunmen from liberally shooting up the buildings in which the Rangers had taken cover.

Several assaults were made during the night and were beaten off with great difficulty. The Rangers received support from helicopter gun ships with night-vision equipment, but their position was desperate by the next morning. Some 18 Rangers were killed and 79 wounded during the fighting.

RESCUE MISSION

During the night, however, a plan was hurriedly thrown together to enter the city and extract the Rangers using ground forces from the U.S. Army, Pakistan, and Malaysia. The Pakistani contingent provided tanks (M48s, which had

ABOVE: U.S. TROOPS UNLOAD FROM A BLACKHAWK HELICOPTER *during United Nations operations in Somalia.*

RIGHT: THE MOGADISHU SKYLINE IS LIT *by weapons fire as U.S. air assets carry out a raid. Helicopters and C-130 gunships were used in the attacks.*

originally been designed and built in the United States), while the Malaysians deployed armored personnel carriers. The rescue convoy, numbering about 100 vehicles with heavy firepower, made its way through the city and successfully extracted the trapped Rangers.

OUTCOMES

It is not known how many Somali insurgents were killed and injured during their attacks on the Rangers or the rescue mission. Estimates of around 800 seem reasonable, though figures upward of 1,000 killed and as many as 4,000 wounded have been suggested. Somali officials claimed a much lower casualty rate. In addition to the U.S. casualties, three men were killed among the Malaysian and Pakistani contingents, and seven wounded. The captured U.S. pilot was eventually released. The "exchange rate" was very high in favor of the U.S. and allied forces as a result of superior training and

ABOVE: LIFE GOES ON: *A Somali child plays amid the wreckage of a U.S. helicopter. The helicopter was shot down during an operation to locate and destroy arms stockpiled by local warlords.*

firepower plus the advantages of defending a good position against an irregular force relying on numbers to gain an advantage. The mission itself was also a success—the targets were captured and brought out of the city as planned.

However, the operation is widely seen as a disaster. The loss of sophisticated combat helicopters to insurgents armed with relatively crude weapons was a shock, and the plight of the Rangers, which could have resulted in the force being captured or wiped out en masse, sent ripples through the U.S. military. One senior officer is reported as stating, "I guess we just don't do cities."

However, in the modern age it is absolutely necessary to be able to "do" cities, and in recent years U.S. military training for urban combat has taken on increased importance. So too has the acquisition of equipment and skills suitable for peacekeeping operations in a fraught and sometimes "warlike" situation where there may not be a clearly defined enemy. Lessons were learned in Mogadishu, albeit at a high price.

REASONS WHY

Operation *Irene* was, on paper, a good plan, making use of mobility, speed, and firepower. However, it became disjointed for several reasons. Poor communications between the forces involved resulted in a long pause while the ground contingent waited for the signal to move in and pick up the captives. It was during this period that the second Blackhawk was shot down.

Overconfidence may have played a part, too. It was not anticipated that helicopters would be shot down in the city, nor that part of the ground contingent would be cut off in hostile territory. Thus there was no contingency plan for a ground-based rescue if something went awry during the operation. The plan that was formulated worked well enough, but the delay was such that many casualties were taken during the 18-hour gun battle fought by the Rangers.

MOGADISHU

3 Blackhawk Super 64 is shot down by an RPG-7. Two U.S. Special Forces snipers are inserted to protect the wounded pilot. They hold out for some time before being overrun.

KEY

◀ U.S. FORCES MOVEMENT

1 Air and ground units move into the city to seize Somali commanders from the Olympic Hotel. Ground units are delayed by barricades and unexpectedly fierce resistance from armed militants. The operation begins to become uncoordinated.

HQ TASK FORCE RANGER

AIRPORT

STADIUM

6 A large force of U.S., Malaysian, and Pakistani troops with tanks and helicopters in support enters the city. The relief force breaks through to the besieged Rangers and successfully extracts them to the Pakistani base at the stadium.

2 Blackhawk helicopter Super 61 is hit by RPG-7 fire and crashlands. A rescue team is able to reach the wounded survivors and remove them from the crash site.

OLYMPIC HOTEL

4 A detachment from the ground force reaches the crew of Super 61 but becomes surrounded and trapped. Large numbers of militants besiege about 90 U.S. Rangers.

5 The trapped U.S. force receives air support from helicopters and holds off repeated heavy attacks despite mounting casualties. Fierce fighting ensues, and by morning most of the Rangers are wounded.

NEW PORT FACILITY

CHRONOLOGY

ANCIENT ERA

The technologies involved in military disasters may have changed over the centuries, but causes such as incompetence, misjudgement, logistical failure and freak events have remained constant.

Kadesh, c. 1274 B.C. (Syria)
The 20,000-man Egyptian army under Pharaoh Ramses II was split by a Hittite

Sea Peoples warrior, 1190 B.C.

army of Muwatalli II, numbering 50,000, and nearly routed. Ramses personally led several counterattacks, pinning the Hittites against the Orontes River and inflicting heavy casualties.

Defeat of the Sea Peoples, 1190 B.C. (Egypt)
A series of victories against marauding tribes known as the Sea Peoples were won by Pharaoh Ramses III, preventing the invaders from subjugating Egypt. Ramses III defeated the Sea Peoples during the Battle of the Delta and the Battle of Djah.

Marathon, 490 B.C. (Greece)
The Persian effort to expand its empire into Greece was thwarted despite their outnumbering the Greeks three-to-one. Firstly, Datis' attempt at a surprise assault on Athens was anticipated by Athenian spies. Then Athenian forces caught the Persians in a pincer movement, leading to a rout of the Persians. 6,400 Persians died against just 192 Greeks.

Thermopylae, 480 B.C. (Greece)
For seven days, a small force of allied Greek hoplites under the Spartan Leonidas held a mountain pass against the Persians of King Xerxes, believed to have numbered several hundred thousand. The Greeks utilized the terrain and extensive training to inflict heavy casualties.

Salamis, 480 B.C. (Greece)
An allied Greek naval force of 300 triremes under Athenian commander Themistocles lured

400 Persian triremes into shallow water and destroyed 200 of them. Many of the Persian triremes were rammed by the Greek ships. Xerxes was forced to call off his invasion.

Carrhae, 53 B.C. (Turkey)
The 10,000 soldiers of Parthian commander Surena killed or captured 34,000 Roman legionnaires led by Marcus Licinius Crassus. The concentrated fire of Parthian archers was followed by an infantry charge which split the Roman force.

Guandu, 200 C.E. (China)
Outnumbered more than three to one, the army of rebel leader Cao Cao slaughtered 70,000 soldiers of Emperor Yuan Shao. Cao Cao destroyed Yuan Shao's supply base, and then defeated his weakened enemy. Yuan Shao fled with fewer than 1,000 survivors.

Chi Bi, 208 C.E. (China)
The combined force of warlords Liu Bei and Sun Quan defeated Emperor Cao Cao in a series of engagements which involved a skirmish at the Red Cliffs, the destruction of Cao Cao's naval flotilla, and the emperor's humiliating retreat.

Adrianople, 378 (Turkey)
The Roman army of Emperor Valens was heavily defeated by the Goths under Fritigern, signaling the beginning of the end for the Western Roman Empire. The Romans, encumbered by their heavy armor, were encircled by Gothic cavalry and pinned against a hillside.

Vouillé, 507 (France)
The Franks under Clovis I defeated the Visigoths, led by Alaric II, who was killed, and gained control of much of southern France, including the city of Toulouse. Clovis crossed the Loire River, his success possibly facilitated by defecting Goths.

MEDIEVAL ERA

The Middle Ages saw a steady transformation in the technology of warfare, such as the introduction of gunpowder weaponry. But other defeats were still caused by armies over-reaching themselves, being outmaneuvered, outfought, and outnumbered.

al-Qadisiyyah, 636 (Iraq)
The forces of the Arab Rashidun Caliphate defeated the army of the Persian Sassanid Empire during the first Islamic expansion. Arab archers and cavalrymen dismounted and charged to victory. The battle resulted in the Arab conquest of Persia.

Kalka River, 1223 (Ukraine)
Near the modern city of Donetsk, the Mongols executed a strategic retreat before turning and defeating their Kievan Rus pursuers, particularly employing heavy cavalry and mounted archers. The victory opened eastern Europe to Mongol invasion.

La Forbie, 1244 (Israel)
Near Gaza, the Mamluks defeated Crusaders and soldiers of the Kingdom of Jerusalem, precipitating the decline of Christian military power in the region. The Mamluks broke the Christian center, killing 7,500 of 11,000 engaged.

Mansura, 1250 (Egypt)
The foolhardy advance of Robert of Artois into the town of Mansura cost him his life and resulted in the rout of his knights by Egyptian forces. Although King Louis IX could eventually claim a tactical victory, the battle ended the momentum of the Seventh Crusade.

Stirling Bridge, 1297 (Scotland)
Scottish forces under William Wallace and Andrew de Moray killed nearly 6,000 English and Welsh troops after cutting off the retreat of the enemy vanguard commanded by the Seventh Earl of Surrey. Wallace subsequently led a raid into northern England.

Battle of Crécy, 1346 (France)
During the Hundred Years' War, the English Army of King Edward III, numbering less than 20,000, defeated a French army more than twice its size under King Philip VI. The English longbow devastated Philip's knights, and the French lost more than 13,000 men.

Nicopolis, 1396 (Bulgaria)
A decisive victory for the Ottoman Turks, Nicopolis marked the end of the great Crusades. Following initial successes, the Crusaders were confronted by Ottoman Turk reinforcements to their front and flanks and were decimated after becoming partly encircled.

Grunwald, 1410 (Poland)
During the largest battle in history involving knights, a coalition of Poles, Lithuanians, and Russians defeated the Germanic Knights of the Teutonic Order. The superior tactics and greater numbers of coalition forces inflicted over 22,000 casualties on the Teutonic Knights.

Fall of Constantinople, 1453 (Turkey)
In April 1453 the Ottoman Turks besieged the well defended Christian city. Using a new Bulgarian cannon, the Turks inflicted heavy damage on the city's walls. After 55 days of siege and on their third assault, the Turks managed to breach the walls of the city, putting thousands of the city's inhabitants to the sword. The great city of eastern Christianity fell to what was becoming one of the most powerful empires on earth.

Knight Hospitaller, 1244

EARLY MODERN ERA

The refinement of gunpowder weapons, the birth of huge standing armies and political infighting all made the Early Modern period an age replete with massive military triumph and disaster.

Prussian infantryman, 1757

Flodden, 1513 (Scotland)
The English army under the Earl of Surrey turned back the Scottish invasion of England by King James IV, while killing or wounding a third of the Scottish forces engaged. Repeated Scottish charges against English troops armed with halberds proved fruitless.

Nagashino, 1575 (Japan)
Modern firearms and defensive tactics employed by Oda Nobunaga and Tokugawa Ieyasu defeated the traditional cavalry charges of forces under Takeda Katsuyori, resulting in the deaths of up to 10,000 of his troops, including more than 50 samurai nobles.

Hansando, 1592 (Korea)
Employing the crane wing formation and executing a double envelopment at sea, the fleet of Korean Admiral Yi Sun-sin destroyed 47 Japanese ships and captured 12, thwarting Japanese ambitions on the Asian mainland.

Sacheon, 1592 (Korea)
Korean Admiral Yi Sun-sin employed a turtle ship for the first time at Sacheon, luring the Japanese into open water. Up to 40 Japanese ships engaged Admiral Yi's 26 vessels, and the Japanese force was wiped out.

Rossbach, 1757 (Germany)
During the Seven Years' War, Frederick the Great of Prussia feigned retreat and defeated the allied armies of the French and the Austrian Holy Roman Empire. Although outnumbered two to one, the Prussians killed, wounded or captured 10,000 enemy soldiers, suffering fewer than 600 casualties themselves.

Leuthen, 1757 (Poland)
The 36,000-man Prussian army of Frederick the Great utilized tactics of diversion and rapid maneuver to defeat the Austrian army, 80,000 strong, under Charles of Lorraine. The Austrians lost more than 20,000 casualties, while Prussian losses were fewer than 6,500.

Yorktown, 1781 (US)
The combined Colonial and French armies of Generals George Washington and Comte de Rochambeau laid siege to the port of Yorktown in Virginia and compelled a British army under Lord Charles Cornwallis to surrender. Defeat at Yorktown caused the British to question continued military involvement in North American colonies.

MODERN ERA

The eighteenth and nineteenth centuries produced military leaders of both shining brilliance and also grievous incompetence, while the conflicts of the twentieth century saw death and destruction on a scale unmatched in history.

Jena/Auerstadt, 1806 (Germany)
The French Army of Napoleon I eliminated Prussian participation in the fourth anti-French coalition for the next seven years. Although outnumbered by more than 50,000, Napoleon's force inflicted more than 45,000 casualties on the Prussians and their Saxon allies.

Chancellorsville, 1863 (US)
The divided Confederate Army of Northern Virginia, commanded by General Robert E. Lee and his lieutenant, Thomas J. "Stonewall" Jackson, routed the Union Army of the Potomac with a major flank attack, facilitating Lee's second invasion of the North.

Isandlwana, 1879 (South Africa)
A 20,000 strong Zulu army equipped mainly with spears and shields defeated a mixed force of British Army regulars and irregular natives armed with modern firearms and artillery. Caught in the open without fixed defences, the 1,500-strong force was virtually wiped out. The Zulus suffered some 1,000 dead and many wounded.

Manila Bay, 1898 (Philippines)
A U.S. Navy flotilla under Commodore George Dewey decimated the Spanish Pacific Squadron during the first major engagement of the Spanish-American War. The Spanish lost seven ships and 161 dead.

Tannenberg, 1914 (Prussia)
During their great victory in the opening days of World War I, the Germans, under Generals von Hindenburg and Erich Ludendorff, encircled and destroyed the Russian Second Army. Russian losses were greater than 300,000.

Somme offensive, 1916 (France)
Conceived as an offensive to relieve German pressure on Verdun, the Somme proved a horror all of its own. The first day of the attack was the bloodiest in the history of the British Army. The offensive gained little territory, and British casualties totaled 620,000.

Battle of France, 1940 (France)
The rapid German offensive through the Ardennes region in May 1940 ended with the capitulation of the Low Countries, the collapse of France, and the evacuation of the British Expeditionary Force from the European continent within weeks.

Operation Compass, 1940–41 (North Africa)
Originally conceived as a five-day raid against Italian forces in North Africa, Operation Compass became a successful offensive, culminating with the British victory at Beda Fomm. The British Western Desert Force killed or captured 118,000 Italian soldiers.

Singapore, 1942 (Malaysia)
Following a two-month retreat down the Malay peninsula, 85,000 British and Commonwealth troops capitulated to a Japanese force of 36,000 in the largest surrender of British personnel in history. The disaster was blamed on an inexperienced commander, poor tactics, and short-running supplies.

Bataan and Corregidor, 1942 (Philippines)
Following a combined battle and siege of more than three months, over 80,000 American and Filipino soldiers surrendered to the Japanese, constituting the largest single capitulation of U.S.-led troops in history. Many of the captives were forced to endure the infamous Death March which followed.

Dieppe, 1942 (France)
In a primarily Canadian operation, Allied forces launched a large-scale raid in the vicinity of this resort town on the coast of German-occupied France and were forced to evacuate after a decisive defeat. Canadian casualties were greater than 3,000.

Operation Bagration, 1944
More than 2.3 million troops of the Soviet Red Army virtually destroyed German Army Group Center during their decisive summer offensive on the Eastern Front. Operation Bagration forced the Germans out of Belorussia and eastern Poland and inflicted more than 550,000 casualties in a two-month period.

Operation Market-Garden, 1944 (The Netherlands)
The combined Allied airborne and land offensive to seize key bridges in The Netherlands ended short of its objective with the destruction of the British 1st Airborne Division at Arnhem. Conceived by British Field Marshal Bernard Montgomery, the offensive was criticized as too ambitious.

Warsaw Uprising, 1944 (Poland)
The uprising of the Polish Underground in Warsaw during the summer and autumn of 1944 was ruthlessly suppressed by the Germans while the Soviet Red Army failed to render aid. More than 150,000 Polish civilians and 15,000 Underground fighters were killed.

Chinese Offensive, 1950–51 (Korea)
Despite warnings of Chinese intervention, United Nations forces were surprised by the sudden onslaught of Chinese troops in November 1950. UN forces were compelled to retreat from the Yalu River, and the Chinese captured the South Korean capital of Seoul before being pushed back.

Private, Iron Brigade, 1863

Page numbers in *italics* refer to illustrations.